God's Blueprint for Building Marital Intimacy

Transforming a House of Sex into a Home of Intimacy

Davil W. Jackson, Ph.D

Forward by Pastor Raymond Turner
Temple Missionary Baptist Church

Writers Club Press
San Jose New York Lincoln Shanghai

God's Blueprint for Building Marital Intimacy
Transforming a House of Sex into a Home of Intimacy

Published by Writers Club Press
an imprint of iUniverse.com, Inc.

For information address:
iUniverse.com, Inc.
620 North 48th Street
Suite 201
Lincoln, NE 68504-3467
www.iuniverse.com

ISBN: 0-595-00697-3

Printed in the United States of America

Foreword

A while back a couple was referred to me for marriage counseling by a friend. After a casual exchange I ask "What's the problem?" After a moment of silence he said "The problem is we haven't had sex in six months."

With this she replied "Pastor, I am not trying to put my husband down, but I am just frustrated with our sex life. What if every time you sit down at the table for a meal, only to find the food gone when you open your eyes after offering the blessing? After a while you just stop coming to the table." As humorous as this may sound to some of you, this is a reality in many marriages today.

One of the problems in this marriage was that the focus was on "having sex" instead of "being intimate." In God's Blueprint For Building Marital Intimacy," Dr. Jackson gives a step by step guideline in "Transforming a house of sex, into a home of intimate pleasure."

This book is truly a blueprint in that it moves from the foundational issues necessary in building intimacy, to "creating the M.O.O.D." which is the love making cycle. It is a book that goes beyond sex in marriage and focuses more on developing a strong spiritual, emotional, and intimate relationship that lends itself to a healthy relationship. A relationship where sex is part of the fulfillment and not the foundation.

If you read this book by starting with the introduction, the table of contents, and skipping to the more "Intimate chapters", you will miss some key information that could be the foundation to a long and fulfilling intimate relationship.

What Dr. Jackson has written here is not a book about making love, but a book about illuminating love through intimacy.

Raymond W. Turner, Pastor

Temple Missionary Baptist Church
San Bernardino, California

I wish to dedicate this book in the memory
of my uncle, Clarence Williams
and my cousin, David Tippins.
Two family members that God took to be with Him,
long before the family was ready to
emotionally and physically release them.

Acknowledgements

Many people helped make this book a reality. Through my life, I have been blessed with people who have made a tremendous impact on my life. It is because of these people that God has allowed to be a part of my life that I am who I am today. It is because of their influence that this book is what it is.

I wish to thank all those who supported and participated in this project through their ideas, time, and energy.

To my wife Beverly and my children, D.J., Ryan, and Alexandria, who sacrificed personal endeavors and consistently provided uplifting support to me in this venture.

I am also very grateful to my parents, Essie and Davil, Sr. who invested time, money, and prayers through all of my lifelong endeavors. You are the example of marriage that set the blueprint for this book.

To my Pastor, Raymond Turner, his wife, Valerie: Thank you for allowing me the opportunity to exercise the gifts that God has given me in the area of marriage and family.

To the members and also the couples ministry of Temple Missionary Baptist Church, San Bernardino, California. I would especially like to thank Roy and Denise Hunt, Valerie Ross, John and Traci Baumann, William and Linda Robinson, Cynthia Wilhite, Monique Mcqueen, Glenda Randolph, Maisha Turner, Walter and Yolanda Taylor, Mike and Joyce Roberts of Harambee Honeymoon Seminars for sharing your personal testimonies and intimate stories.

To Aqua Gayden, Kimberley Grant, Chandra Payne, and my other colleagues in Los Angeles County for their encouraging words, and insightful thoughts.

And lastly, to personal family friends, Michelle Stafford, Magali Williams, M.A., Psychology, Bradford Leviege, M.A., Education, and my Aunt, Joyce Bell, M.P.A., for their eyes, ears, editorial skills and positive contributions.

Contents

Introduction

The purpose of a blueprint is to provide step by step instruction from the beginning of a project to its conclusion. In every aspect of growth, there are steps for effective management. Problems result when there is a deviation from the plans.

In the development of a relationship, the stages are: meeting (that first moment when eye contact is made and the heart goes pitter-patter), dating (when the two individuals begin spending time together and making decisions with their hearts), and engagement (when a decision to marry has been made and thinking should be done with the head). Marriage, sex, and children then follow. This is the relationship blueprint that has been preached for many years. Yet, some attempt to take the steps out of order, not based on needs but on desires.

I have spent several years working with Christian as well as non-Christian relationships and counseling singles preparing for marriage. The same question usually presents itself at one time or another. "What is the secret to staying in love" or "How do we keep the candle of intimacy burning?" I always present the same answer: Communication and an ever-increasing effort to please the other, often without concern for your own needs.

One of the most difficult parts of a relationship is intimacy and romance. In the beginning, everything is great. You've found that person who can meet your needs and you're in love. Your heart beats fast, you're on the phone until all hours of the night, you can never get enough of each other. Then, you get married, and "all hell breaks loose" in every room of the house, especially in the bedroom. The desire for intimacy fades, how do you get it back?

Communication and an Ever Increasing Effort to Please the Other, Often Without Concern for Your Own Needs

With all the day to day stresses of work, finances, children and other outside activities, it can be difficult to maintain intimacy and romance. Failing to spend time intimately can result in a lack of emotional and physical support, which can leave a partner neglected and searching for fulfillment outside of the relationship.

I've been married for 16 years to Beverly, and we have come to realize together that keeping intimacy alive requires a great deal of communication. It took nine years for reality to set in, to realize that maintaining intimacy was similar to building a custom home. Not every couple in a relationship is equipped with the same needs and wants; that's what makes it a custom home. It's never a good practice to compare your building ideas with those of others; everyone has different taste.

Being a man and spending time around men, in every conversation women became the topic. The men would talk about the various things their wives or girlfriends did intimately, which would make the other men wonder why they don't get the same treatment from their women. In most cases, these men were lying just to make their home appear better equipped than the other. It's important that you view your relationship as a home that you design with the taste of you and your partner in mind.

There are different designs for every couple, based on personal choice, but the building process is the same. When building a home, there are five things required to assure strength: (1) a strong foundation, (2) a sturdy frame, (3) a wall for security, (4) a roof for safety, and (5) a strong lock to keep out all intruders. The same principles apply when building a home of romantic intimacy.

The purpose of this book is to reach couples concerned about strengthening intimacy in their relationships. The intent is to focus on emotional intimacy. The idea is not for him to remember how he felt during sex, but for him to remember your showing emotional signs of appreciation after sex. The idea is not for her to remember his skill during physical sex, but to remember his wonderful approach prior to sex with flowers, music, and a nice planned evening. This sounds like a fantasy, but it doesn't have to be. Desire begins in the mind and the body follows through. In the next several chapters, it is my intention to help to rekindle a lost fire.

Chapter One
...Till Death Do us Part

What a frightening statement!! I've heard some give the age old advice, "marriage is no bed of roses." Now, if marriage were really a bed of roses, then the husband and wife would be sleeping on thorns. One of my closest friends of 25 years states, "I'll never get married. Everyone I know who is married is now divorced, except you Davil." This friend is basing his rationale for not marrying on observations of failures. Everyone looks at the divorce rate and listens to negative reactions from those who have tried marriage and failed. Its even worse when it occurs in your immediate family or you are the child of divorced parents. These thoughts can produce fear and a reluctance to marry.

If Marriage Were Really a Bed of Roses, the Husband and Wife Would Be Sleeping on Thorns

Scary, isn't it? But I'm happy to say that is doesn't have to be scary if the proper foundation is created. When the focus is directed toward a combined effort with one mind, soul, and spirit the fear can be alleviated. The idea of marriage has changed tremendously over the years, and the original principles that held relationships together in the past have been replaced with superficial values created for needs of convenience. When I counsel couples, I have yet to hear them talk about how they can make the other happy. It's usually "what I want."

However, marriage can mean happiness for those men and women who have decided to unconditionally love each other and commit to God in a monogamous relationship focused on meeting each other's needs. It's not a term that should bring fear, but a challenging joy.

I enjoy counseling individuals who have met what they think is their "soul mate." There was a young lady who had met a nice gentleman, and she was excited and happy. She bragged about how good looking he was and his athletic features. He sent her flowers and called her throughout the day to say he was thinking of her. The idea of marriage came to her mind. She worked around others who were married, had homes, cars, children, a dog—the whole family lifestyle. What she didn't understand was that she was an outsider looking in and saw current relationships in the developed stage. She did not have the knowledge of what it takes to achieve the family lifestyle she desired. I encouraged her, but warned her not to allow her fantasy of love to cloud her vision of reality.

In every relationship, especially after marriage, that fantasy can come true. Making it come true is similar to deciding to build your own custom home; the thoughts are in the mind and the ideas are on paper. But when the actual building begins, there will be circumstances that come between the building process and your plans. You realize that what was in your mind takes hard work and may seem impossible to build. In a relationship, one often forgets that there are two people with different ideas. These differences will hamper the building process unless both parties move from the fantasy into the reality stage.

When Beverly and I got married, I had fantasy ideas and so did she. My fantasy was that I would be met at the door with kisses of gladness. There would even be an occasion where I would come home, and there would be various items of clothing leading from the door to the bedroom in an intimate setting. Or maybe I would often receive little gifts that would signify that she was thinking about me. But once into the marriage, I began to understand that my fantasies were just that—fantasies. My ideas included what I thought marriage was to be, and did not consider what Beverly thought. Beverly is intimate and loving, but did not share my fantasy. I was selfish in expecting her to read my mind without realizing that she had her fantasies too. And, was I meeting her needs?

As a counselor, I can always detect who is causing the most problems in a relationship, based on finger pointing by the other partner. Based on my experience it is the finger pointer who needs the counseling. In building a true home of intimacy, there are two persons involved. When there is a problem, there should be two persons involved in correcting any misunderstandings.

The success of a marriage depends on the consistent strengthening and empowering of each other. God found favor in marriage such that He related the relationship between Jesus and the church as an example of marriage. *"Wives, submit yourselves unto your own husbands, as unto the Lord. For the husband is the head of the wife, even as Christ is the head of the church; and he is the savior of the body. Therefore, as the church is subject unto Christ, so let the wives be to their own husbands in everything. Husbands, love your wives, even as Christ also loved the church, and gave himself for it, that he might sanctify and cleanse it with the washing of water by the word"* Ephesians 5: 22–26.

God uses the husband as the foreman in the building process. I remember going to work with my father who was a truck driver. On the loading dock, there were laborers, and the foreman was responsible for the activities on the loading dock. Not only were the laborers working, but the foreman was working just as hard. I recall the foreman assisting them to get the job done efficiently. When the job runs smooth, the foreman gets the credit for leading the workers. However, when the job is not getting done, the boss holds the foreman responsible and does not blame the laborers. It's his job to make rational decisions in the best interest of his family, and supervise them in all issues they may face. No matter how tough the job may become. In the eyes of God, it's not winning the race that is important, but finishing the race. When a man chooses to take on a wife, he cannot run back home or abandon ship with fear. God will hold the husband responsible even if he walks off the job and leaves the building incomplete.

The same principle applies in building a home of intimacy. God has given the husband the responsibility for ensuring a productive and meaningful job in the marriage relationship. It's the man's responsibility to operate with a level head and to keep constant communication with God.

While God puts a heavy responsibility on both the man and the woman, the heaviest is on man. He is to love his wife, just has Christ loved the church. Christ was a sacrificial offering; the sins of the world were destroying the eternal soul of man. Christ was sent down from heaven and considered a bridegroom who took on a bride, which was the church. The church was in trouble and full of shame before God. However, it did not matter to Christ how dirty and filthy the sins of the church were, he sacrificed himself and created a marriage union based on spiritual principles of love and commitment. To build and empower a spiritual intimate relationship, the same principles apply. In an intimate relationship, there should be a division of roles in terms of what works in the best interests of the relationship. There is a husband and wife who live on my block. I always see her mowing the lawn and caring for the yard without her husband. I inquired, and she stated that her husband is better at chores in the house, and she worked better on the outside. There was no disagreement; whatever was necessary to keep the home together and keep them both happy was what they did. I always inform couples in counseling that whatever it takes to make life easier for the other should be done. There has to be some kind of understanding between the two.

Therefore, "till death do us part" is only frightening to those who choose to build using their own personal plans. But, those who have chosen God as their building developer, Jesus as their building contractor, and the Holy Spirit as their spiritual inspector for guidance, can expect intimate benefits from their labor. *"Except the LORD build the house, they labor in vain that build it" Psalm 127: 1.*

Take Time to Think:

Do you have any "...till death do us part" fears? What are those things that you and your partner fear the most? (Parental divorce, finances, identity problems, etc.) Consider those fears that may prevent a commitment to marriage. Discuss them with your partner to obtain support and understanding. If your concerns are a real struggle, talk to a counselor, and most of all take it to God in prayer and ask him to guide you through those fears.

Chapter Two

...A Single Word to Single Men (Identity)

Men, stop looking for that perfect woman who can cook all your favorite meals, wash your clothes, and bear and raise your children. Look for someone who loves you as a respectful, caring man led by God. Too often men look for a woman to fill a need, not realizing that they may be lacking what it takes to fill the woman's need. God has designated someone to fulfill our needs, but that person may not fit our fantasy. Perhaps God is saying, "I want you two to work together to build your relationship. If she had to do everything, then there would be nothing left for you to do."

A single male looking for a partner has the perfect opportunity to ask God to work on him for someone else. I have a friend who is single, and he asked me to pray that God would send him a companion. I happily stated I would do him a better favor by praying that God would prepare him for a companion. Many times, singles overlook themselves when looking for others. As a man, one of the most single important thing to possess is your own "identity." Your identity determines who you are and what you are about. Identity should be reflected in goals, accomplishments, and future achievements. Your identity gives you sole possession of yourself. But, when you allow your identity to be controlled by others, they can take it away at anytime, leaving you to struggle for your dignity.

As a Man, One of the Single Most Important Goals Is to Possess Your Own Identity

I recall a couple in counseling. The husband did not work and did not bring any male identity into the relationship. The wife was the breadwinner, paid all the bills, furnished the apartment, and performed the tasks required to keep a home together. The husband simply sat at home watching sports on television without acknowledging any responsibility on his part. During counseling, the husband became upset when his wife would gain the upper hand by reminding him that she worked, she paid for everything and, without her, he would not have anything. This statement angered the husband, but the wife had the leverage. Furthermore, she owned his identity. Even when he would choose to leave, he would always return because he had nothing internal upon which to build.

Just being born a man does not an identity make. So often, men want to be respected simply because they are male, but lack the qualities needed for building an "identity." Yet, a stable relationship must be equipped with a man with a positive identity. He must be sure of himself, and bring those positive qualities into a relationship as a leader. Children born into a family need a strong structure in which to develop their identity. Children will develop their skills based on what is viewed in the home. If a son views his father sitting home doing nothing, lazy, and lacking family responsibility, he will think this is the norm and carry the same skills into his own relationship.

Building an "identity" requires a total self-assessment, often without validation from others. As humans we tend to avoid giving compliments for fear that it will "go to one's head", or people will become "stuck on themselves." If there is no personal inner belief, there will be no outer respect. As a man building an "identity," it is your responsibility to seek those things you need to enhance your identity. This means using the vision that God has provided for you and your own wisdom. Having a strong identity will help prevent inner insecurity and the intimidation that often challenges men. Without an identity, you will always feel the need to compete, which is not always necessary. As a man who is slender, weighing about 135 lbs, I attend the health club three times weekly. It's interesting to observe the bodybuilders going out of their way to try to intimidate me by lifting well more weight than I can. But what's intimidating to them is my strolling over to the chin-up bar and completing three sets of 20 chin-ups. They look amazed at my ease, not realizing that a man with a developed identity can't be intimidated. Once you've developed your identity, then you can search for someone with whom to share it. Don't go looking for an identity, bring one to the table.

The cycle of men without a responsible identity needs to begin with seeking God in prayer, and asking Him to create within you a new heart, and the right Spirit. The right Spirit will yield to the right direction. A man with an identity through Jesus Christ will not be afraid to lead his family, care dearly for his family, and most of all pray for his family.

Too much time is spent looking and not enough time searching. Looking only focuses on the surface; searching produces a deeper desire to reach an inner understanding. Looking causes visual attraction, searching produces deep emotional attraction that goes deeper than the eyes. I have heard many interesting conversations regarding married couples, especially the old statement, "What do they see in each other? I wonder what attracted them to each other?" There is a simple answer to these questions. The attraction is usually something that the person on the outside cannot see or understand. It is only visible between the two parties involved in the relationship.

When it comes to searching for a partner, know who you are first and then what kind of partner will further enhance your identity.

A Chance to Look into You:

To further understand your personality and write down at least 10 personal strengths that are apart of your personality that can be an asset to others and used to strengthen yourself (i.e. Communication, leadership, humor, etc.).

1.
2.
3.
4.
5.
6.
7.
8.
9.
10.

Chapter Three

...A Single Word to Single Women (Purpose)

Being a Godly, single woman has its struggles. Likewise, being a Godly married woman has another set of trials. While I am single, it is important for me to earnestly study God's word and seek His purpose in my life. Through studying, I will learn the proper steps necessary to handle any situation. If I feverently study God's word while I'm single, my relationship with Him will only become stronger, and prepare me when He sends my husband. It is also important for me to have a Godly married mentor. The purpose of this person is to help guide and teach me as I take steps to become a Godly wife. Living life today, whether single or married, has its fair share of problems. God has given each of us the tools we need for successful living. It is our responsibility to grab hold of these provisions and live for Him.   *Maisha*

Single women, stop looking for Mr. Right. I believe that a Mr. Right has entered every woman's life at one time or another, but for some reason there was something found wrong with him. He was either too short, or fat, or skinny. His hair was the wrong texture, his skin the wrong color, either too dark or too light. You didn't like his car, he didn't make enough money, he was too educated or not educated enough.

These are some of the many excuses I've heard from women who are still looking for Mr. Right.

As a woman, you need a "purpose." Know yourself first. If you don't have a relationship with yourself, it will be difficult showing your God-sent partner how to relate to you. Don't ever allow a man's identity to dictate your purpose. But, don't allow your purpose to dictate his identity. A relationship based on purpose and identity will produce fruitful results because it means that you have a valid reason why you are involved. Whether or not you know it, to become emotionally or physically involved with someone without a purpose will eventually produce an unwanted identity and purpose that some women never seem to shed.

Why do women feel that they can't survive without a man? There are women who believe that "half a man is better than no man at all." The problem with this belief is that if you have no purpose, you'll probably end up with the half that is empty and not the half that is full.

> *I must confess, when I was in my twenties, I had no idea that GOD was preparing me. For what, I really didn't know. Then when I was in my thirties, I still did not know GOD was still preparing me. But now I have turned forty, I know that GOD has been preparing me all this time for my husband. He has shown me my purpose, and this purpose is to wait on Him to bring me my husband. And when we do get together, my husband will be happy to say that he has found "a good thing."*   *Josey*

After awhile, it gets old viewing the same relationship scenarios time after time. Usually a woman will change her life plans and purpose based on a man. The need for a purpose keeps you focused on what you need to do for yourself. Without a direct inner purpose, you began to compromise those things that were once precious to you. I always try to encourage teenage girls to develop their inner self without the need for male validation. Don't allow what you are to be given to you, but know that you are beautiful, know that you are special, and know that you are your number one priority. Always remember: TO THE WORLD, YOU MAY NOT BE GOD'S GREATEST GIFT, BUT YOU ARE GOD'S GREATEST GIFT TO YOURSELF. As a gift from God, it's important that you treat yourself well. God placed you here. Now, take the time to adorn yourself with yourself. But this can't be done without a purpose.

To the World, You May Not Be God's Greatest Gift, But You Are God's Greatest Gift to Yourself

Remember, when God sent Jesus to marry the church, He wasn't looking for a perfect church because God created human beings with flaws and imperfections. It's interesting how years later, that nerd that you turned away went on and found a companion that focused on the gift inside the package and not the wrapping. When you allow the wrapping to excite you, and there is no concern about the contents it can often bring disappointment. When you meet a man, don't be afraid to pick up the box and shake it. Challenge him with your purpose, desires, needs and requirements. He may have great wrapping, but the contents may not meet your needs. His contents may be empty or the opposite, too full of unnecessary junk. It's always puzzling to me to hear about people who have fallen for bait and switch scams. They will purchase an appliance way below market value on the streets, only to get the box home and discover its filled with bricks. When searching for a partner, you must be careful and not fall for the smooth words, soft voice, or just simple availability. You may find that he is filled with burdens that will not only weigh down your physical nature, but can jeopardize your walk with God.

"Beloved, believe not every spirit, but test the spirits whether they are of God;"! John 4:1. The importance is not to just watch the tree, but pay attention to the fruit it bears. And always remember that if the test of your love is predetermined by sex, then its really okay to fail that test.

If he bears something other than what God has required for you, then that fruit may not be healthy for you. If God sends him, not only will the fruit be spiritually, and physically healthy, but will also be sweet to the taste.

When you meet a man, don't be afraid to ask questions, to inquire about his feelings on love and marriage. If your questions make him uncomfortable, take that as a red flag, and put that package back on the shelf. Little do you know that it may have been a returned item with defects and simply rewrapped for someone else; it doesn't have to be you.

If the Test of Your Love Is Predetermined by Sex, Then Its Really OK to Fail That Test

In the process of looking for a companion to help you build your home of intimacy, you have to be aware of how God would have you build, not what you choose to build. Upon finding who you think is the right person, communication is essential, especially spending quality time talking and listening to each other. You need to share your goals about building a house of romantic intimacy. Ask for God's guidance, and be willing to accept His answer, whether or not it's something you want to hear. Don't ever rush to the altar to say "I do" knowing that he can't.

Chapter Exercise:

To further understand yourself as a women, write down at least 10 personal strengths that are a part of your personality (i.e. friendly, submissive, quiet, etc.)

1.
2.
3.
4.
5.
7.
7.
8.
9.
10.

Chapter Four
...In the Beginning

The institution of marriage was ordained by God Himself. Genesis 2: 22 puts the whole order of sex and marriage into perspective. It was God's design that the man and woman would come together and meet for the purpose of curing loneliness. Sex was considered a secondary celebration as a signifying of two partners becoming one flesh. Through the process of time and historical changes, sex has become the primary focus of the relationship and marriage possibly running close third after several children are born.

Now let me began by saying, I didn't make the rules and I wasn't there of course. And many would wonder why would God play such a trick on the human race. Why would God create man and give him all the physical and visual desires, give him a brain, and give sight? Then turn around and create woman with so many different physical features that keep men's head turning and often making statements such as: "If God had created anything more beautiful he probably kept it for himself ". There is a woman that I know who always ask me questions about the strangeness of men when it comes to women. As we were talking one day, she thought it was strange that when a woman walked by, all a man needed to do was to move his eyes if he really wanted to see her. But why, she said..does he have to go through so many physical movements and reactions? Almost causing car accidents, making full body turns and running into walls and doors.

The questions are often asked, Why God, why would you create such works of art in human flesh and then finish it with an understatement. "DO NOT HAVE SEX UNTIL YOU ARE MARRIED, IT IS CONSIDERED FORNICATION" What is fornication? Sexual intercourse outside of marriage. Sounds cruel doesn't it, but God in His foresight and wisdom realized that sexual intercourse is more than just a physical act, but can produce emotional damage to the physical body, and spiritual destruction to the soul. Sex and intimacy was established as a pleasurable experience between a husband and wife. However, intimacy can be shared by two persons without sexual intercourse. As a Christian couples counselor, I've found that most problems related to sex are due to a lack of foundational friendship through intimacy. Intimacy is often interpreted as sex.

In my personal opinion, I believe that God designed sex for married couples so that they couldn't compare their partners to anyone else. This contrast and comparison brings intimidation and causes insecurity in a relationship. This view of thinking is definitely old fashion and not new age. But when we speak of building a home of marital intimacy, it wasn't God's design that you start building from the inside out.

No Need to Practice Safe Sex…If Safe Living Is Practiced

In today's society, everybody is concerned about sexually transmitted diseases and if their partner has any sexual secrets. It was God's design that His people need not worry about STDs if they live according to His word. Even now, my wife and I get laughed at because we were virgins when we got married. Nevertheless, it's something that we continue to be glad about. The concern today is with passing out condoms and teaching teenagers how to use them, without teaching them that sex out of the designed order puts the heart and mind at risk. There are many teenage girls who feel pressured into sexual participation and, once rejected by the boy after sex, have problems with self-esteem. They have sacrificed their emotional stability for physical gratification, not understanding that physical gratification was for the benefit of the boy. The intimacy has been taken out of sex and young men and women don't understand the consequences. However, when safe living is taught as a way of life, sex resumes its role as an expression of intimacy within the relationship.

Chapter Five
Intimately Homeless

"*Nevertheless, to avoid fornication, let every man have his own wife, and let every woman have her own husband. Let the husband render unto the wife her due; and likewise the wife unto the husband. The wife hath not power of her own body, but the husband and likewise also the husband hath not power of his own body, but the wife. Defraud ye not one the other, except it be with consent for a time, that ye may give yourselves to fasting and prayer, and come together again, that Satan tempt you not for your incontinency*" I Corinthians 7: 2–5.

> "My husband has hurt me by ignoring me and put me through so much that I can't bring myself to want to make love or have sex with him at all. I have needs as a woman, but I find other things to do to keep busy, like kids, job, exercise, church, or just walking to keep my mind off things, and I'll be so tired that, when I go to bed, I'll go right to sleep."   Judy

> "I can remember when our first child was born. There were times when my mind would reflect on the intimate moments that were in the past. I would always wonder why things had to change. There were times when I began to feel insecure with myself and my wife no longer wanted me intimately. It wasn't always the sex I needed, but the personal attention that would make me feel special at that moment.

Maybe a small gift, or a card, or anything that would show she really cared for me and appreciated me as a husband and father"   Jack

It may be shocking to discover that many partners involved in a marriage live in a house, but are actually homeless. The word of God provides instructions for both the husband and wife to do all in their power to render intimate sustenance to each other. The writer recognizes the fact that humans have emotional and intimate desires. To fill these desires, God requires that a man and woman come together in holy matrimony for the purpose of fulfilling these needs. When a man and woman become as husband and wife, they are suppose to give their bodies to each other without selfishness. And when couples refuse to give themselves to each other without any agreeable reason, or lose that comfort zone of the one flesh feeling, one partner may began to suffer from an intimate need. Just as when physical hunger occurs, the whole body can suffer from its pain. When an emotional and intimate heart is empty and feels hunger pains, a partner will sometimes go to any extreme to have that hunger filled, even if it's outside of the marriage. When this occurs, that partner becomes what I've described as intimately homeless.

To be intimately homeless is to have a recurring feeling of emotional hunger and to have no means to have it fulfilled. Homeless individuals wander and continuously search for a home. The problem is that along the way, they often venture off-track and have problems finding their way back. Individuals that suffer from intimate homelessness search for a fulfillment, often outside of the relationship to whom ever will fill the need. Once they've stumbled into a homeless shelter of the adversary, the task becomes more and more difficult to find their way back to their partner. It's very important that partners reassure each other and keep the intimate pantry stocked with compliments, reassuring thoughts, and other intimate desires that fill your partner's needs. Remember to fill your partners need, not just yours.

It becomes very important for couples to pay close attention to their partners emotional and intimate needs.

Never Say What Your Partner Needs to Hear, Say What They Need to Feel

All individuals want to be made to feel comfortable and loved in their relationship. To deny that privilege will often leave a mate searching to fill that hunger in other areas when it is not readily available at home.

SIGNS OF BEING INTIMATE HOMELESS:

1. A feeling of loneliness, even when your partner is living in the same house.

2. An intense hunger for emotional validation, intimacy, and inner security.

3. A constant searching to fill the intimate need from whatever source available.

4. Allowing someone other than your partner to temporarily fill the hunger for Intimacy.

5. Not being willing to give 100% of yourself in the relationship.

WAYS TO KEEP YOUR PARTNER INTIMATELY FULL:

1. Always take time to view your partner with positive thoughts. Take time to notice your partner and listen carefully in conversations. Always recognize your partner's ability to care for you.

2. Always be mindful that gifts can be given for any occasion other than just holidays. Gift giving should be based on spontaneous feelings for your partner.

3. Take time to ask your partner how he or she feels about your relationship. You may feel comfortable, but your partner may feel a sense of loss in an area and be afraid to tell you. Pay close attention to your partner's response. NEVER SAY WHAT YOU PARTNER NEEDS TO HEAR, SAY WHAT THEY NEED TO FEEL.

4. Give and receive with the same enthusiasm as when you first met. Dating should never end. Search to satisfy to the utmost and never give up trying.

5. Be mindful of activities outside of the relationship taking too much time from your partner.

Filling the Need:

This project requires careful consideration, honesty and thinking. Are there any areas in your relationship where you feel an intimate hunger that is not being filled by your partner? Or, if you know you've been neglecting the need of your partner, think about your feelings and discuss them with your partner. If you have a problem with communicating verbally, try writing a letter, sending a card, or just asking if their intimate appetite is being filled.

Chapter Six
The Purpose of Building a Home of Intimacy

1. Marriage was designed by God to meet the first problem of the human race: LONELINESS (Genesis 2: 18–22)

God created man and saw that everything He had created prior to man had a companion. Therefore, God created woman as a helpmate and companion. Foundational importance in any relationship is to view your partner as a vital part of yourself with a goal of satisfaction. It's disturbing for me to hear about couples who have a disagreement and spend days, weeks, and sometimes months sitting in the same room, sleeping in the same bed, and even attending the same church, but not speaking to each other. If there is no conversation within the relationship, there is loneliness. If there are issues in your relationship, it doesn't matter whose fault it is or who apologized the last time. Somebody should recognize the need to be a peace-maker for the building process to continue. I've heard that "make-up sex is the best sex." That's exactly what it is—"sex," a physical release based on built up emotions due to a lack of intimate communication. God designated that a man and woman would cherish each other and continue to edify each other with love.

What Adam Needed Was a Companion Not Based on Visual Appreciation, But on Physical and Emotional Appreciation

Before building can take place, a relationship has to have a common thread that pulls the partners together. It's difficult to build a relationship when only one has the desire to build it to its fullest.

It was interesting to me how when God decided to create woman without incorporating or involving any of man's ideas. God put man to sleep and thus proceeded to create a female being designed to fit mans need, not his want. What Adam needed was a companion not based on visual appreciation, but on physical and emotional appreciation.

If Adam were involved in the creating of his companion, he probably would have let his physical nature override what was really important in a partner. But thanks to the wisdom of God, He left man out totally and gave them both something in common to build from: AND THAT WAS EACH OTHER'S LACK OF KNOWLEDGE ABOUT ANYTHING ELSE BUT EACH OTHER.

2. Marriage was planned and decreed to bring happiness, not misery. *"Marriage is honorable in all, and the bed undefiled, but fornicators and adulterers God will judge" Hebrews 13: 4.*

Stress and unhappiness in a relationship can only produce an incomplete relationship with a lack of satisfaction. When a marriage is based on misery, intimacy becomes a mundane physical process that brings no satisfaction or growth. Human life requires a balance to run smoothly, and the purpose of a home of intimacy is to establish that balance. If there is stress in the place of employment, and no peace in the home, there is no balance, and intimacy will suffer. This is especially true for the woman, due to the emotional nature of sex for her. If her mind is occupied with other issues, it prevents her body from experiencing total tenderness.

It was God's idea that a man and woman would come together for the purpose of pleasing each other and no one else. Throughout the building process, it is important to relate to each other with happiness in mind. Sound impossible? Some might say that no couple in their right mind can't always be happy. While circumstances within the marriage can present misery and resentment, one can keep focused on one's partner. If there is love and caring for each other, this will create happiness even in difficult situations. A simple conversation of hope and support, without deliberate harmful intentions will strengthen intimate thoughts and provide internal feelings of security.

3. Marriage means oneness in the fullest possible sense, including intimate physical union without shame. *"Therefore shall a man leave his father and his mother, and shall cleave unto his wife; and they shall be one flesh. And they were both naked, the man and his wife, and were not ashamed"* Genesis 2: 24–25.

Learning about intimate sexuality does not always occur in the family setting. Even when homes are filled with a variety of how-to books, children are not taught about sex in its proper perspective. They are taught how to do it, but never how to use it in the perspective it was meant. Sounds silly, how do we use sex properly? It's the same as teaching a teenager how to drive a car. A parent just doesn't hand over the keys without giving some type of instruction on how to use it properly. What is sad is that parents spend more time preparing their teenager to drive a car than discussing the emotional and spiritual issues important to intimate sexuality in the context of marriage.

Oneness can mean simply being together and not necessarily for the purpose of intimate satisfaction. Oneness is a growing process, requiring an understanding of how partners witnessed affection in their homes as children. My father owned his own trucking business and would frequently be out of town. My parents would affectionately greet each other when he left and even more upon his arrival. However, my wife's family was different. Her parents were much older, and she never really witnessed much affection as a child. There was a need to for us to build our oneness based on an understanding of how we were, without taking our disappointments personally. I had disappointments because I felt neglected. She had feelings of disappointment because she felt unable to fulfill my needs. By learning to understand each other, I became more patient and she became more comfortable in expressing affection.

A couple desiring to build a home of intimacy should evaluate their purpose for coming together. Think about it, is it out of a personal, selfish, lustful gain? Or, are you sincerely interested in providing companionship, fellowship, while creating an intimate partnership?

Intimate Building Break:

Why have you chosen to build a relationship with your partner? After understanding God's principles for creating relationships. Spend quality time with your partner on this exercise, exchanging ideas on attributes, personal knowledge, skills that will help you both to understand your purpose in building your home of intimacy.

HIS	HERS
1.	1.
2.	2.
3.	3.
4.	4.
5.	5.
6.	6.
7.	7.
8.	8.
9.	9.
10.	10.

Chapter Seven
Intimacy

"A true relationship must have a growing rising love. Intimacy involves physical, sexual, educational, intellectual, emotional, and spiritual dynamics. In reference to sex, styles of intimacy and ability to show affection and sensitivity are necessary. A healthy and loving relationship requires work, quality time, commitment, love, and communication."
Ginger

"There are many things my man could say to me that could stimulate me without his touch. But I find that when he is able to communicate his feelings about our relationship, including those things about me that makes me feel good, honesty must play an important role: saying what he truly feels about me and not just saying things that sound good. Expressing himself in a strong passionate manner is also a plus. Passionate conversation with romantic overtones always seems to stimulate me and put me in the mood."
Mary

A lack of understanding of the difference between sex and intimacy has caused problems in relationships for many years. These terms separate the male and female attitudes towards sex.

The average man looks forward to having sex, while the average woman looks forward to receiving intimacy. Sex is a physical activity, while intimacy can involve physical, and emotional activity.

Depending on the individual, intimacy can range from a soft stroking on the back, to spending time in a park on a swing, to passionate sexual activity. Women, please don't get mad at your man; men were not taught how to be intimate, only about sex. Intimacy is a learning experience for every man, and it requires a woman's patience and guidance.

Men are taught to "get in and get out." We were not taught to get you in the mood, get in, then pay attention to your bodily reactions, focus on your breathing, attempt to please you, then get out, and then spend time afterwards cuddling once we're out. Women know what they want, and need to take time to tell their partner and not blame him for not knowing. Assume nothing, even if you've been together for 10 years. Has he spent the last 10 years playing trial and error, or have you spent time during sex gently guiding him through those things you desire? If you have and it still hasn't worked, be patient and never give up hope.

When It Comes to Sex, Men Were Taught to "Get in and Get Out"

One of the greatest gifts a man can give to his partner is the gift of making love to her mind first. When love is made to her mind first, the rest of her body will follow with expected and unexpected pleasure. In other words, "when her mind is tender, her body will surrender." The mind is the control tower for the body. A man well versed in and totally in tune with his partner will always strive to stimulate her mind first. When her mind is stimulated with careful words filled with passion in a secure emotional environment, said in a soft voice feeding her intimate inner desire, she will surrender her body more easily than simply being told, "I want to do it."

When Her Mind Is Tender, Her Body Will Surrender

Likewise, the greatest gift a woman can give her partner is her total self without prerequisites or inhibitions. To understand the principles of a spiritual and fulfilling sexual relationship requires consistent thought, creativity, and communication. It makes no sense for a woman to wait many years before she tells her husband that she has not been intimately satisfied. Both partners must exchange ideas that enhance the pleasure that God had in mind when He created this beautiful design of oneness between two people.

The Greatest Gift a Woman Can Give Her Man Is Her Total Self Without Inhibitions

In the area of intimacy and sex, there are myths that cause both men and women to feel self-conscious. I talk to women who speak of changing themselves in many areas. They say that it's to please themselves, but I find that hard to believe. Why would a woman in love with herself need to increase her breast size, spend thousands of dollars in weight loss programs, or feel that she has to measure up to a perfect "10"?

One of the biggest myths for men is penis size. Does it really matter how big it is or its length? I can remember conducting a workshop on sex and posing that question. Only one woman quietly raised her hand to say that she thought size was important. I used the following example to explain my philosophy on the subject.

When I started playing golf, I had problems hitting the ball off the tee with my driver. I had observed other golfers on the course who seemed to be using drivers bigger than mine and felt that the size of my club wasn't sufficient. I bought a mid-sized driver, but still couldn't hit the ball. Then I traded up to a bigger driver, and I still couldn't hit the ball. Finally, I went to the biggest, but somehow the ball still wasn't going anywhere. Another more experienced golfer whom I had been playing with was amused that every time he saw me, I had a different driver. He advised me to go back and get the smaller driver. I complied. He took it, set himself up, and hit the ball about 250 yds. He then informed me with great wisdom, "Son, it's not the size of your club that counts, but your technique in using it." I've come to the same conclusion in the area of sex and intimacy. Men should not be preoccupied with the size of their penis, but rather their technique. It takes more than the old "plunging in and out", but an actual skill that requires observing your partner before, during, and most especially, after sex.

It's Not the Size of Your Club That's Important But the Technique Involved When Using It

Intimate Project

Trading Intimate Building Ideas:

Do you have any intimate assumptions? Are you expecting anything special in the area of intimacy that your partner may have no knowledge? This project requires that you both list intimate assumptions for the purpose of understanding and fulfilling each other's intimate needs.

HIS	HERS
1.	1.
2.	2.
3.	3.
4.	4.
5.	5.

Chapter Eight
A House *vs.* a Home

W hy a HOME OF INTIMACY and not a house of intimacy? There is a big difference between a house and a home. The biggest difference is what goes on within the walls on the inside. When God developed marriage, it was His purpose to bring warmth, security, and comfort to both partners. "Home is where the heart is." To build a home of marital intimacy, the heart must be the focus. It is the job of the husband to provide security and nurturing so that destructive forces do not enter the home. When issues arise within the home, to depend on his wife to resolve household issues is not Gods design. God placed him as a leader for the purpose of maintaining a balanced home. The wife's job is to support her husband, and with her support he should do all in his power to make her lady of the home. The three together will help establish and create a home of marital intimacy: God the Creator, man the laborer, and woman the decorator.

The Difference Between a House and a Home Is What Happens on the Inside

To understand the importance of building a home of romantic intimacy, let's look at the flip side. There are other places where sex is performed called houses. There are houses of prostitution, whore houses, and even houses of ill-repute. True, sex is within the walls of these houses, but there is no love, no warmth, no heart. It's simply a business arrangement between two people who don't know each other intimately, and it does not have the purpose of meeting intimate needs. The meeting in the house is for the purpose of sex, and it's over with no ties or affection. These are houses in which there are immoral practices.

In Hebrews 5: 22, God compared the marital relationship to the church. If it's one thing that church members hate, it's an unclean church. When church members come to worship, they prefer a comfortable, clean building. Often, in the beginning of a relationship, there is some cleaning and personal refurbishing that should be done. Past hurts and disappointments unrelated to the present relationship need to be addressed prior to building a home.

At the beginning of a new relationship, the concern is directed toward outer appearance. However, the real problems stem from the inside. In a physical house, there is always at least one pest the structure has to be protected from. This pest is usually termites, and most termite problems are left from the previous owners. Termites destroy from the inside. It may take several years for their damage to appear. Often they cannot be seen, but the damage can be recognized. This is why it's important that the home's inner structure be examined from time to time.

In a relationship, there may be internal damage slowly destroying your partner, and the only way to recognize it is to spend time observing and communicating with concern. It is also important to try to fix the problem. Internal problems also can cause physical problems and erode wellness.

A House of Intimacy Can Never Be Built
If You're Never at Home to Build It

If there is too great a focus on the physical house, then it is difficult to make it into a home. People today appear more concerned with the appearance of prosperity and achieving the great American dream than spending the time developing an inner connection within their intimate dream. There are many relationships that look beautiful on the outside, but are not beautiful inside.

One woman shared with me that her husband didn't understand her beyond her material needs. She needed more of his personal time and intimate attention. His concept was that he was the man and that his job was to work, provide a home, a car, and financial support for his family. He felt that his wife was being ungrateful. However, the husband couldn't comprehend the fact that his wife had an intimate need that couldn't be fulfilled by anything or anyone else but him. He needed to recognize that his home of intimacy needed his attention. This husband didn't understand that a "HOME OF INTIMACY CAN NOT BE BUILT IF YOU ARE NEVER AT HOME TO BUILD IT!!!"

Chapter Nine
Following the Blueprints

With the idea of building or constructing a structure, there are a set of pre-designed instructions called "blueprints". Blueprints act as a guide that should remove any doubts and questions as to how the building should be built.

The word of God (Bible) is a Christian couple's blueprint for building a home of marital intimacy. Never deviate from God's pre-designed plan for your relationship. Never rely on your own knowledge, because personal knowledge is too full of opinions based on feelings and emotions. What ever the subject regarding relationships, there will always be different ideas. But when the blueprints are followed, it leaves no room for second guessing. The instructions to whatever questions are available, and they require simple obedience. God's blueprints are designed to provide needed directions. Leaning on human knowledge can ruin the harmony for the laborers.

When God's Blueprints Are Followed, It Leaves No Room for Doubt

"Trust in the Lord with all thine heart, and lean not unto thine own understanding. In all thy ways acknowledge him, and he shall direct thy

paths. Be not wise in thine own eyes; fear the Lord, and depart from evil"
Proverbs 3: 5–7.

In an effort to build the best home of romantic intimacy, a couple must spend quality time on a daily basis studying the blueprints. Concentrated study will insure that the laborer won't neglect any detail of the building no matter how big or small the task.

In Christian counseling, I find that there is lack of personal quality time directed toward building by the blueprints. The strength of a building is through the pre-designed instructions.

A strong building also requires an exceptional amount of energy, not to mention necessary sacrifices. As a relationship develops, there are many things that will interfere, some intentionally, and others unintentionally.

Studying the blueprints together is designed to keep a couple on one accord building in the direction with the same mind. If the harmony between a couple can be broken down, the building process can be hampered and sometimes abandoned and left incomplete. If a relationship in the intimate building process is left incomplete, there will always be someone passing by who becomes interested in the incomplete structure. Whatever the subject or the issue that comes between a couple involving building their relationship, never leave your partner emotional unattended. It's just the same as leaving a house unattended or abandoned. Eventually, someone will move in and take up residency.

One main importance is that both partners build with the same ideas in mind. Human nature between a man and a woman can really cause confusion in many areas of the relationship. And it's really nothing personal against any sex, but God created a major difference in each. But unless you take the time to obtain a clear understanding of your partner, you will often build in opposite directions. This is very common among couples in several areas. In the "he does his thing, and she does her thing" relationship,and neither knows in what direction the other is going. He's attempting to build a pool room, and she attempting to build a sewing room. Both are so preoccupied and exerting energy within their own building needs, but neglecting the whole purpose of why they are together in the first place. This has caused many couples to have to tear down what was started and rebuild a second time, considering each other and following God's blueprints. To maintain a nurturing relationship, it is also important to spend time with other couples who have the same desire and building achievements. Entertaining burdens from other couples and especially singles who seem to always have problems with the opposite sex can create a hardship on the building process. It's real interesting that the person who talks the worse about your relationship is usually the person that wishes they were in your shoes.

I know that the word of God says that we are to bear one another's burdens, but not in the context where it causes unnecessary hardships in your relationship. I'm a firm believer that a couple has to act on issues that promote nurturing in their relationship, and not encouraging destruction.

God has given the proper materials, but it requires work to put them together. As a counselor, it gets old when a couple comes in for counseling and they are given common sense instruction designed to bring them together based on biblical ideas. They cannot find the time to act upon it, yet they would rather sit in an office for one hour and pass negative information about each other week after week. There is no excuse for this. If God doesn't build the house, the laborers labor in vain. A couple is laboring in vain when they neglect the blueprints and ignore sound instructions. It's very important to spend time daily in God's word, individually and as a couple. When a couple allows God as their guide, He will construct your relationship into something beautiful: not only for yourself, but as a witness for Him.

DAILY EXERCISE: As a couple, take 10–15 minutes daily for prayer and time in some type of spiritual devotion. The purpose is to bring you both together on committed spiritual level. Coming together will help your relationship gain spiritual and physical strength needed during the intimate building process.

Take out the Trash Daily

I find that when a couple would rather spend time slinging trash, the home becomes messy. The inside will never get clean if the trash keeps piling up. The more the trash piles up, the more unhealthful the living conditions. Let's face it, when it gets too bad, somebody is not coming home, or the property may become inhabitable. I hear couples in counseling, who have gone so far piling trash upon each other, day after day, year after year, until they feel that they could never live again under the same roof. Personal attacks and intimate hurts stink, and cause serious damage to the relationship. It is important to call on God to assist you in clearing the trash from your relationship. There is never too much trash in your relationship that God cannot help you clean, if only you have the desire to follow His blueprints and spend the time laboring.

A good rule is to never dump personal trash on outside friends or family. When physical trash is taken out, there is a can designed for household waste where it can be picked up and permanently dumped. It would be inappropriate to dump the trash out on the front lawn because it would not only destroy the beauty, but the trash would still remain. However, when a couple dumps their trash at the altar through prayer, God can cleanse them with an odor of forgiveness. But when a couple chooses to dump it elsewhere, their personal trash may become recycled by others and possibly come back to stink up their home of intimacy through other methods.

Following the blueprints will encourage divine direction and spiritual guidance, as well as provide an opportunity for God's glory and blessings to illuminate your relationship. It also will restore confidence in the institution of marriage. Your relationship will stand as a light shining on a hill to other relationships and to those who fear "till death do you part."

Time to Dump the Garage:

Is your home cleared of emotional and intimate garbage? Is there an unclean odor of hurt feelings or sadness due to a disagreement? Take the time now to try and resolve those disagreements. Don't allow the odor of sin to destroy and present an unhealthful living condition in your home of intimacy. Take time in prayer together and ask God to help you clean up your intimate home.

Chapter Ten
Dressing for the Job

" *Put on the whole Armour of God, that ye may be able to stand against the wiles of the devil. For we wrestle not against flesh and blood, but against principalities, against powers, against the rulers of the darkness of this world, against spiritual wickedness in high places. Wherefore, take unto you the whole armor of God, that ye may be able to withstand in the evil day, and having done all, to stand" Ephesians 6: 11–13.*

A wedding ceremony is one of the most beautiful occasions, for which much time, money, and energy are invested. The bride is gorgeous and all attention is focused on her. When she walks in, everyone stands in amazement. The groom stands dressed elegantly and with confidence as his bride strolls down the aisle approaching him. The crowd looks on as they take the vows that will determine their future, no longer as individuals, but as one flesh in the name of God.

In Ephesians, Paul encourages every believer, including those involved in a relationship, to equip themselves and to cover-up for the purpose of defending each other against outside forces. Paul states that the best defense against troubles that will plague a relationship is the Armour of God. I've watched builders as they have diligently worked on building a home and observed them wearing clothing designed to withstand their rugged task. They were covered from head to toe in clothing designed to protect their body. If they were only half dressed, they would leave part of their body unprotected which would effect the rest of their body if injured. If a worker chose to cover his feet and left his head uncovered, something could fall from above without warning. These men recognize that building a home requires commitment, work, sweat, and a constant commitment to the job until its completion. In a relationship, a couple must understand that they have to accept their vows and each other with 100% commitment. God requires that relationships participate in the building process by putting on Armour to stand against the trickery of the devil. Unless a couple realizes that their relationship is going to be attacked from time to time, they will have a rude awakening. A couple must realize that the reality of the world often appears to distort the wonderful things that God has placed His seal of approval on.

When the Wedding Attire Comes Off, the Wedding Vows Should Stay on

Many relationships have been torn apart because of lack of spiritual protection. Just because a couple has given their life to Christ and have come together in a Christian ceremony it does not mean that their relationship is exempt from outside troublemakers. The ceremony does not make a marriage. It's after the ceremony where a marriage is made. When a couple is dressed in wedding attire, they are given a level of respect outwardly. No matter how the guests may feel about them inwardly, they will stand in respect for the bride and congratulate the groom. But, when the wedding attire comes off, the wedding vows should stay on.

"To have and to hold, from this day forward, so long as you both shall live." The protective dressing is in the vows, and by only living by a portion of them will leave portions of your marriage exposed. You can't dress your partner with jealousy, follow them around by spying, or show a lack of trust. But you dress them with the fruitful ingredients provided in the word of God. Dressing for the job is not based on outward appearances, but inward defensiveness. A couple has to always continue to defend themselves against societies principalities. It's not the size of the diamond in the wedding ring that dresses its wearer, but what is the heart of the presenter. The diamond is not the protective attire, but its round symbol of an unbreakable love is the real protection. People will tempt your commitment and love to each other, and if Satan can cause confusion with just one partner, the whole marriage will suffer.

Its Not the Size of the Diamond That Dresses a Marriage, But the Size of the Giver's Heart

Wives, when you were eying your husband, didn't it seemed that nobody wanted him. However, one day you stopped and talked to him, discovered that you had something in common, and started spending time together. Did you then find that the other women also began to find him attractive and tried to gain his attention? Husbands, wasn't it after you shared with your friends how attracted you were to your wife, that some of your friends who never paid her any attention, now began to do so? That's how the trickery of the devil works. However, the grace of God put you both together and the same will sustain you.

Prior to meeting Beverly at her church, I had approached other women, who ignored me. But God knew exactly what I needed and put Beverly in my life. After we became a couple, some of the other women now approached me and informed me that they were interested in me from the beginning, but I just didn't give them enough time, and now wanted another chance. Human nature will approach your relationship, often not to help it along, but to hinder it. Society is full of unhappy people who may have not taken advantage of opportunities given to them, and to view another's happiness, provides them sadness and disappointment.

God Knew Exactly What I Needed When He Put Beverly in My Life

After we had announced our engagement, among all the congratulations, there were a few negative remarks by those who were miserable and sought to pass that spirit on. A woman approached us and informed us of how difficult marriage is and wondered whether we could make it work. I was happy to inform her that our marriage would be founded on the "ROCK of Jesus Christ."

A good example of armoring your relationship is a conversation I had with Beverly after we both began working for the same company. I had been employed there for three years prior to her employment. I was a messenger who traveled from office to office delivering mail. I have an outgoing personality and became known by many employees in several different locations, the majority of whom were women.

Most of them knew that I was happily married because I spoke often about my wife.

Its Very Difficult to Hit a Moving Target

Nevertheless, I didn't overlook human nature. I told Beverly that, once she began working, she should be careful because people may attempt to say something to discredit our relationship. The purpose of this conversation was to guard our relationship against any forces seeking to destroy our happiness. As luck would have it, I happened to be out to lunch with a group of female employees, and another female who worked with my wife observed my presence. When this woman returned to work, she informed my wife that she saw her husband out to lunch with a "bunch of women." My wife smiled and said, "Yes, I know. He told me last night that he would be out celebrating a birthday."

The only way to fight against foes and "messy" people is to stay dressed in God's amour and never take it off. Always continue to abide together.

Move closer to God day by day. It's very difficult to hit a moving target, but when a couple stops growing together, they leave their marriage wide open as an easy target.

Chapter Eleven
Tools Required for Building

Have you ever experienced a time in your relationship where it seemed you and your partner were going nowhere? Did you sense that you both were going through the motions, but you were missing something? You tried and tried, but you just couldn't put your finger on where the stalemate existed. Don't give up. It may not be you that's the problem. It may be the tools you are using to build and enhance your relationship.

The Quality of a Job Is Often Predicated upon the Quality of the Tools Used

In a relationship, tools are important. What's even more important is how the tools are used and that they are used for the right job. If you are attempting to build a home of intimacy with improper tools, it's like trying to turn a screw with pliers. It will work, but with difficulty and the job will be of lesser quality, and you may damage the screw.

Laborers working on a building wear a tool belt around their waist. They recognize that they need to keep their tools handy. As couples work together to build their relationship, they need to keep their tools near. They cannot wait until a tool is needed and then search for it. Once it is found, the damage could be worse.

The tools required for building a home of marital intimacy can be found deep within the heart. The problem is not locating them, but asking God to put them into your spiritual tool belt and give you the ability to use them. When God created man, He provided everything that was needed to build the relationship. However, we must study and develop the skills to use the tools adequately.

"But the fruit of the spirit is love, joy, peace, long-suffering, gentleness, goodness, faith, meekness, self-control; against such there is now law. And they that are Christ's have crucified the flesh with the affections and lusts. If we live in the Spirit, let us also walk in the Spirit. Let us not be desirous of vain glory, provoking one another, envying one another" Galations 5: 22–26.

A couple cannot equip themselves with the necessary tools. However, through the Holy Spirit, the tools can be provided, along with the instructions. There are basic tools that every couple should possess in their marital tool belt:

1. **Communication**. Many loving couples never talk about sex and intimacy. They often haven't developed a comfortable sexual vocabulary or the ability to talk about their lovemaking. Lack of communication can cause a home of intimacy never to be built adequately, and it will forever remain only a house.

It is important to never assume anything. Many couples think that their partner should be able to read their mind. If there is an issue in your relationship, it must be discussed. I had been reading my newspaper at the table for many years. After about 12 years, Beverly said to me, "Hey, let's make an agreement. How about you not reading your newspaper at the table, and I'll let you read it in bed at night." I happily replied, "I won't read it in bed, but I definitely won't read it at the table again during dinner." I was puzzled as to why she allowed this issue to go on for so long without informing me. She said, "Well, I would think that you should have known it was rude to read at the table with me sitting there. My response was," Well, I didn't think it bothered you; you never said anything before." Many issues could be avoided if only we learn to communicate when we feel violated or mistreated. It's damaging to get angry at your partner and when your partner asks "what's wrong" you say, "you know." In some cases, we do know. But this response takes too much time in producing a resolution. The longer it takes to solve problems, the longer it takes to complete the building.

Another reason why communication is not used effectively is a fear of hurting one's partner, especially in the area of intimacy. Couples will spend many years together engaging in unsatisfying sex, but are afraid to tell their partner for fear of hurting their feelings. Extramarital affairs are sometimes explained by one partner not wanting to hurt the other's feelings, so desires were fulfilled elsewhere. Men are especially victims of this because we feel that we don't need help, advice, or guidance. Men take their sexual performance personally, and to discuss it may be a blow to his ego. However, It would hurt my feelings more if Beverly didn't tell me that I wasn't satisfying her needs. This is why it is important to communicate and talk about what goes on intimately in your relationship. There is a Christian and edifying manner in which to communicate your needs to each other without hurt feelings and resentment. Edifying communication ask you both to think before you speak. *"Let all bitterness, and wrath, and anger, and glamour, and evil speaking, but put away from you, with all malice; And be ye kind one to another, tenderhearted, forgiving one another, even as God, for Christ's sake, hath forgiven you" Ephesians 4:31–32.*

2. **Knowledge.** A couple must be comfortably knowledgeable about each other when attempting to build their home of intimacy. Time must be taken to study responses, attitudes, and feelings in an effort to fully satisfy each other intimately. It is important to understand that this process takes patience and a willingness to be knowledgeable about your partner.

"In the same manner, ye wives, be in subjection to your own husbands that, if any obey not the word, they also may without the word be won by the behavior of the wives" 1 Peter 3: 1.

In like manner, ye husbands, dwell with them according to knowledge, giving honor unto the wife, as unto the weaker vessel, and as being heirs together of the grace of life, that your prayers be not hindered. Finally, be ye all of one mind, having compassion one of another, love as brethren, be pitiful, be courteous. 1 Peter 3: 7–8.

3. **Honesty**. Dishonesty can prevent a house from becoming a home of intimacy. It is important to share feelings in an effort to improve. Many concerns can remain hidden and can cause the building process to come to a sudden stop. If there is an area in your relationship that needs to be addressed, you owe it to your partner to share this information. Honesty gives your partner an opportunity to share in the issue, as well as an opportunity for both of you to share in the solution.

4. **Creativity**. Romantic creativity is often left out of an occasion for intimacy. Creativity takes thought, time, and energy. When you first met your partner, you thought of creative ways to spend time together. The best gifts were given, you were never short of words, the term "I love you" was never said enough. Those wonderful nights out, weekends away, and flowers, cards, and poems sharing your intimate thoughts and feelings bolstered your relationship. Now that you are in a relationship, all those wonderful things that brought the two of you together for the purpose of building are no longer present. When building a home of intimacy, the same creative material it took to start the building are needed to complete the building.

Creativity seeks to build with the ever evolving materials to produce a home of intimacy that will produce endless desire. Creativity won't allow children or any other interruptions to jeopardize a couple's intimacy. Children can get blamed when there is a blocking of intimacy, but this is simply an excuse due to a lack of creativity. Parents must creatively work around blockades in an effort build more effectively.

5. **Discipline**. There are so many things that seem to take control of a couple's time and energy, including thoughts, stress, children, work, and even church. Lack of discipline on the part of one partner can make the other feel guilty for wanting to be involved intimately. In most relationships, intimacy becomes the "when we have time" activity. It is important to recognize that what is necessary is to maintain a strong, sturdy intimate household. When you really think about it, activities outside your home of intimacy are usually for the benefit of someone else and not necessarily for yourselves. Thus, you must know when to say "no" to others.

6. **Respect**. In the area of intimacy, a husband and wife must give honor to each other. Ephesians states that wives must be submissive to their husbands. It also states that husbands are to love their wives as they do themselves. To be totally comfortable with intimacy, respect must be given unconditionally without the fear of producing intimidation. Never allow the practice of submission to make you feel less than a woman or feel that it takes something away. Through submission, a wife not only yields herself to her husband, but also unto the will of God. *"Wives, submit yourselves unto your own husbands, as unto the lord. For the husband is the head of the wife, even as Christ is the head of the Church; and he is the savior of the body. Therefore, as the church is subject unto Christ, so let the wives be to their own husbands in everything. Husbands, love your wives, even as Christ also loved the Church, and gave himself for it, that he might sanctify and cleanse it with the washing of water by the word; That he might present it to himself a glorious church, not having spot, or wrinkle, or any such thing; but that it should be holy and without blemish. So ought men to love their wives as their own bodies. He loveth his wife loveth himself. For no man ever yet hateth his own flesh, but nourisheth and cherisheth it, even as the Lord the church; For we are members of his body, of his flesh, and of his bones. For this cause shall a man leave his father and mother, and shall be joined unto his wife, and they two shall be one flesh. This is a great mystery, but I speak concerning Christ and the church. Nevertheless, let everyone of you in particular so love*

his wife even as himself; and the wife, see that she reverence her husband"
Ephesians 5: 22–33.

This scripture is often taken out of context by men and ignored by women. This due to that one word "submit." God's blueprint gives instructions for a wife to submit to her husband. God intended for wives to submit to their husbands because, in God's divine order He gave man attributes related to leadership skills. If a man chooses not to follow Christ and merely follows his own mind in the building process, his partner will begin to have doubts about his leadership capabilities.

The Equity in My Home of Intimacy Goes up 100%

God admonishes wives to give husbands the respect due them, and God gives a husband direct instruction to honor his wife. By honoring his wife, he honors himself. When a wife looks and feels good, this is often a reflection of the husband. When my mother would attend church, she was strong, confident, happy and always well dressed. The women in the church would often comment that her husband must be taking good care of her, simply because of how good she looked. I love sending Beverly flowers at work, the equity in my home of intimacy goes up 100%, not only with Beverly, but with her co-workers who become even more excited than she. To honor one's wife means that you honor yourself.

To give respect means a sincere desire to receive the same. Just because the husband is the head of the household does not mean that he can do everything well. God gave both the husband and wife skills. One purpose of a relationship is to recognize which partner has certain skills that can benefit both partners.

Chapter Twelve
Unequally Yoked

Be ye not unequally yoked together with unbelievers; for what fellowship hath righteousness with unrighteousness? And what communion hath light with darkness? 2 Corinthians 6: 14

Those who have chosen to accept the principles of God's word on building a home of intimacy have instructions to seek out a companion who has also not decided to conform, but has transformed themselves by the renewing his or her mind. The substance of 2 Corinthians not only applies to yoking within the marriage relationship, but involving yourself with anyone, whether platonic or monogamous, that will spiritually, mentally, or physically hinder your spiritual walk. I've been asked on several occasions "how does one know when God has sent a partner?" My response is to remind them that if God sends a companion into your life, they will not challenge you to live against God's word. Why waste time trying to build a serious relationship when there is the possibility of "irreconcilable differences?" It's never in the best interest of any relationship for one partner to become yoked to a "stumbling block" instead of a "solid rock." Do you ask God to yoke you with someone who is going somewhere? Or do you make your own choice and yoke yourself with someone who gets in the way while you are trying to go somewhere?

It's Never in The Best Interests of Anyone to Become Yoked to a "Stumbling Block" Instead of a "Solid Rock."

One key to building toward a strong and fruitful relationship is to yoke yourself with someone who has the same destination in mind. Too often, individuals, who are born again Christians, will yoke (by their own choice, not God's) themselves emotionally with others who are not.

God recognizes that the transformed thinking processes of those whom He has brought out of darkness into His marvelous light, are different than the thinking processes of those who remain in spiritual darkness. As a Christian, one's outlook of life is based upon faith and dependence on God and His divine blueprint, coupled with a commitment to following His will.

To be yoked or married to someone without the same spiritual principles can cause an imbalance in the relationship. The unequally yoked syndrome has caused many relationships to be built on a "teeter totter" foundation. Imagine two people who have decided to get married and build a home together. One may feel that it is easier and less expensive not to lay a firm foundation, and there is no need to dig, survey, or check for environmental defects. However, it is important to dig and survey the ground because it may be contaminated, toxic, or dangerous. How many relationships have come together without the couple surveying themselves, only to discover that one person has anger management problems or has no concern about the other's well being. There are even those who have chosen to build on a earthquake fault! If you build on a fault, you are subject to earthquake devastation. You know it's dangerous, but you never know when an earthquake might strike.

This same idea applies in relationships; there are some who have built their relationship on a fault line. They are been warned with red flags but have ignored the warning signs. When things get shaky in the relationship, they both begin fault finding and blame each other instead of seeking help through prayer and counseling to establish a building focus. Nevertheless they simply build without any forethought in mind.

The other person in the relationship may think, "I've been taught to build differently. I was taught to dig down to the solid rock (pray and consult God first) and to lay a foundation of cement (seek God's will, not mine). "Yet, both may decide that, as long as they have started building a home of intimacy together, the foundation does not matter. After all, the foundation is something that is under the house, out of view. The other person may even agree that love will keep them together and that they will eventually come to a balance in the future.

Does this scenario sound familiar? The house is built; it looks beautiful on the outside. However, outside forces beat against the house and the foundation begins to sink. They've become stressed; they have no interest in intimacy, joy or happiness in life. The point is that many Christians have chosen to build with non-believers and continue to struggle on a foundation that has an unknown shift. They never know what to expect from their partner. Think about whether you are involved in a relationship that is unequally yoked. Are you trying to build your home of intimacy by yourself?

A testimony from an unequally yoked relationship: *Can two walk together, unless they are agreed? Amos 3: 3*

I could fill a library with words of warning against becoming unequally or unevenly yoked. Can two walk together? I had to come to grips with who the two were. I always assumed that this scripture meant my companion and myself, but it really hit me hard to realize that this scripture should have turned the light bulb on my relationship with the Lord. Could I really walk with God and disagree with Him at the same time? If I truly loved the Lord and was in a deep love relationship with Him, how could I so blatantly plunge into a relationship that was so obviously out of His will?

Consider a farmer, who had a field to plow. He would take the time to consider the kind of field and he would have to be careful to match the right oxen to get the job done. He would consider the size, the temperament, and the compatibility of the two who would be yoked together. He certainly wouldn't put two stubborn oxen together; he'd have overturned carts all over his field. He wouldn't mis-yoke them in size, that would make one have to pull harder than the other. He'd take time to observe and put together the team that could pull the plow and he would yoke them evenly.

Every ox I've seen needed a farmer to match it evenly with another and put the yoke on them. Jesus prayed in John 17 that we might come to know Him. If I really knew Him, like I said I did, I should have known that he is my farmer. I should have known that , as my farmer, it was His place to put together the matched team that could pull the load evenly. I should have known that He was the One to put the yoke on. Sadly, there are many individuals who yoke themselves unevenly. We often think of the other person as the cause of the yoke being uneven. I had to be honest and admit that the cause was me. My relationship with the Lord was uneven. I professed Him , but I wasn't willing to obey Him. I should have been willing to wait on the Lord, knowing that, as a loving farmer, He would put together the best team. I have had to live with the consequences of becoming unequally yoked. My advice to anyone considering marriage is to read John 17. If it doesn't click, read it again. Keep reading it until the light bulb comes on. We often feel comfortable marrying someone we think we know a lot about. What about God Almighty? Do we really know Him? If you really know Him, you would trust Him, and if you trust Him, you obey Him. When I married, I wasn't concerned with knowing God. I was more interested in Him picking up the overturned carts I knew were coming. I knew what I was doing wrong. My pastor and friends begged me to wait. I am still suffering from the consequences of my outright rebellion and stubbornness. I really think that I have spent more time choosing what I wear than I did on choosing a lifetime companion. The scripture says "He that findeth a wife have found a good thing and obtains favor from the Lord". Making that decision to disobey God cost me more than I was willing to pay. As bad as the marriage was, the divorce was even worse. The thought never entered my mind the day I was married that, four years later, I'd be

*serving my spouse with divorce papers. And that's my point. You don't know
what to expect anytime you stray out of God's will.* Rhonda

Making That Decision to Disobey God Cost Me More Than I Was Willing to Pay

Chapter Thirteen
Love *vs.* Lust

The term LOVE is often used out of its proper context and in the process, has confused many. Love, when used in the proper context, can bring joy, fulfillment, and light to a life in darkness.

True Love Is Not Comprised of the "Kissing of Lips" and the "Grinding of Hips"

Love is often misunderstood or confused with lust. Instead of saying, "I love you", some mean "I lust you." Love is more than just a physical feeling shown through an erect penis or a welcoming vagina. It's more than the "kissing of lips" and the "grinding of hips." Love focuses on depth; lust focuses on the surface.

"It was love at first sight" is a phrase I've heard often by two people who really don't know each other, but need a reason to substantiate their rationale for coming together in a relationship. It was probably "lust at first sight," the physical attraction that usually brings two people together. It's human nature to show some form of lust, but past a point, the lust should fade into a solid feeling based on feelings unrelated to the physical. What makes it worse is when one really feels that he or she is in love and doesn't recognize that it is lust. Even worse is when you know your partner is in lust and you use that feeling to try and turn it into love. Lust is a momentary feeling, while love is a lasting and embedded desire. It is unexplainable to others, manifested as a form of majestic illumination from a couple.

True love is not a hidden experience and has no special place to flirt, no special occasion for gifts from the heart, will say I'm sorry without finding fault. True love knows how to meet a need before the need is even needed.

True love can be seen by others. This love can be seen through facial expressions, bodily movement, and look of contentment. I can always tell when a couple is happy in their relationship based on their overall attitude, appearance, and expressions. There could be a hundred women in a room, but when she walks in his presence, there is special twinkle in his eyes. And when that gleam appears from him, she will counter with a smile.

True Love Knows How to Meet the Need Before the Need Is Even Needed

There was a young lady who was broken hearted because the man she was involved with decided to end their relationship. He gave some excuse which was, of course, not satisfactory to her. They were both confused. She was in love, or so she thought, but he was definitely in lust. This young woman would clean his apartment, cook, wash his clothes and, of course, provide access to sex. Now she felt hurt, betrayed, and lost. She couldn't eat or sleep, and she cried continuously.

After listening to her, I was sorry to inform her that he would be back. "No", she said, "he's going to move out of the state and start fresh somewhere else." I again regrettably informed her that he would be back. By then I had her attention, and she wanted to know why I was so sure. "Why wouldn't he?" With you, he didn't have to work hard. You expected nothing from him and, if you did, you were probably not serious about it. Right now he's probably thinking of how easy he had it with you—a built-in housekeeper, cook, and someone for sex. Just wait until that physical need in him arises, that desire. His penis gets erect at thinking about what you both did in bed and how handy you were to have around. I know this sounds cruel, but it's usually the truth. He'll come back just wanting to talk to you. You'll entertain his warm apology. He'll say, "I love you", and whoop, there it is. You make some demands, he'll agree. You make-up by having a great night of wild lustful sex. You won't be making love, because you can't make something that you never took the time to create. "No," she insisted, "he is not coming back." Her mouth was saying one thing, but in her heart was a different story.

After giving this young lady this whole scenario, the worse part was that it happened just like I said it would. To further demonstrate the imbalance, it appears that she wanted to start building the relationship toward something comfortable; he did not. However, he was willing to enjoy the comfort she was building. For whatever reason, she decided to start building without him, probably thinking that he would eventually join her and they would come together as in a romance novel or a fairy tale. However, what usually happens is that the one party just sits and observes, while the other works, and just reaps the benefits without lifting a finger. As a counselor, I don't always want to be right about certain situations. I like to warn individuals about what's going to happen in order to mentally prepare them. I understand that it is difficult to be alone, but some make great sacrifices just to feel loved, but never receive the satisfaction they crave.

Anything Less Than Your Best Is Not True Love

When building a home of romantic intimacy, true love is the foundation and binds the structure. The structure includes church, work, children, family, and finances, which need to be bound together for a sturdy relationship structure. God requires that we constantly bind our relationships by giving our partners the best that we have to offer. Anything less than your best is not true love. When you use cheap material, it causes problems, and you have to replace these materials. To bind the structure requires the grace, mercy, and blessings of God. Human nature can cause one to fall out of love, but a strong spiritual nature will cause an outpouring of love upon the relationship.

To achieve love requires not just one type of love, but three types of love: Agape, Phileo and Eros. All three stand together for the purpose of bonding a relationship with strength, durability and longevity.

The Three Levels of Intimate Building Material

The Foundation: Agape Love—Is immediate love by choice that is brought into the relationship because it has no dependence on feelings. It is a love of action, not emotion.

The Frame, Walls, and Roof : Phileo Love—A cherishing of tender affection, always expecting a response. It is a love of sharing, communication, and friendship.

Interior Decorating: Eros Love—A love of emotional feeling, romantic, passionate, and a yearning to become intimately and/or sexually involved.

The point I am trying to make is that a sturdy home of marital intimacy cannot be adequately built to the comfort of a home with just a foundation of love. It also needs a frame, walls and roof. And again, what good is a home that is empty on the inside. A true "till death do you part" relationship requires more than just Eros love (sex), or just agape love (unconditional acceptance), or just phileo love (friendship). They all work together to assure that the relationship is built and prepared to withstand any circumstance that should come against it. The following chapters will focus on how the three kinds of love work together in building a home of romantic intimacy. I will say that patience is very important when building a physical home, and when it comes to building your home of romantic intimacy in your relationship, the same patience should apply. Read the material through your eyes, not your partner's eyes. Think about what can you can do to create an intimate home, for yourself and for your partner.

Think about it:
Is It Really Love or Lust?

Why do you love your partner? List specific reasons as to why you feel God has chosen your partner as a building companion. As an extra assignment for couples, write your feelings on a card or letter and give it to your partner. Whether you are a writer or not, the purpose is to become totally dedicated toward building a stronger relationship. You'd be surprise how one line of special attention can build strength.

Chapter Fourteen

Laying a Foundation of Substance (Agape Love)

"*Love suffereth long, and is kind; love envieth not; love vaunteth not itself, is not puffed up. Doth not behave itself unseemly, seeketh not its own, is not easily provoked, thinketh no evil. Rejoiceth not in iniquity, but rejoiceth in the truth; Beareth all things, believeth all things, hopeth all things, endureth all things*" I Corinthians 13: 4–7.

Does your idea of love come close to anything like the descriptions above? Did you ever think that real love required so much energy? The real surprise is that there is more required of the giver than of the receiver. This means, however that if both partners gives the same measure of love, they will receive the same measure of love.

AGAPE LOVE is derived from a Greek term meaning "everlasting love." That is an unconditional selfless love that will go to any length to attain the well being of its object. This is how Jesus Christ loved the church and gave Himself for it. To build an intimate home, a couple must build upon Jesus Christ's principles of love. Agape love is a forgiving love. When disaster occurs, the walls are destroyed, the roof caves in, and the interior decoration is destroyed. Agape love presents a foundation on which to rebuild.

The purpose of a solid foundation can be understood through this personal testimony:

I was married 17 years before I really understood the importance of agape love in my relationship. I was unsaved and, even though my wife professed salvation, she didn't live it. We were living without a stable foundation: spiritually, emotionally, mentally and, especially, sexually. Our intimacy was of a physical need and not an act of love and pleasure. Thus, I began to seek pleasure outside of my marriage. We both were out of control, especially me. I had no knowledge of what direction to take to bring things back into focus. We visited counselors, but their help was only a surface bandage. Down inside, I really thought that my marriage was over, and there was no need to waste any more time trying to rebuild it. After much pressure, I finally went to a Christian marriage seminar. However, I didn't go for myself. I was only accompanying my wife so she could find out what her problem was. I, on the other hand, went for the purpose of fishing, swimming and since we'd have a hotel room, definitely plenty of sex.

I accidentally came into contact with one of the speakers who began to minister to me about God's plan for marriage and my role as the husband. After attending some workshops, I prayed and discovered God's plan for my life. I became saved and began trying to rebuild my marriage according to the principles of Agape Love. From that point on I began to understand God's will for me as a husband and it was to put my wife first in my life. Everyone and everything else became unimportant.

I now understand how to truly love my wife. I understand that it's my job to be her spiritual leader. I understand that it's my job to ensure that she has a happy home at which to arrive everyday. I now understand that when we are intimate, her needs come first, and then mine. I truly understand the real meaning of agape love because it has enabled my wife and I to rebuild a stronger home of intimacy. And it was even more beautiful when my wife showed agape love by forgiving me for all the terrible and insensitive things I had done to her in the past. She now began to accept me as a husband, a family leader, and a unselfish, sensitive lover. Jason

This testimony demonstrates how effective an agape love foundation can assist in rebuilding a marriage. Jason and his wife are true witnesses of how a love that is dug deep within the soul will remain even when things on the surface may have been torn down.

The attributes of love, as described in I Corinthians 13: 4–7, leave no doubt as to how Agape love is manifested. It is manifested in commitment, acceptance, giving, support, and patience.

There was a Sunday School teacher who, in the middle of a lesson used his wife as an example of how Satan (the devil) works. He explained that he woke her up at 5:00 a.m. that morning because he wanted her to fix breakfast for him and the family. She declined, and he felt that she had the devil in her that morning. While it may sound like his wife was insensitive, in actuality, his wife was experiencing a difficult pregnancy and lacked the physical energy. This man took her response as insubordination and disobedience to the will of God as a submissive wife. If her husband had been practicing agape love, he would have understood that love seeketh not its own, and is not easily provoked. He should have understood her physical condition and shown love through seeking her needs, not his own.

Agape love would have led this man to bring breakfast to his pregnant wife in bed, to have knelt down by her side, waiting with eager mind, heart, and spirit to provide services for her.

"A Building Is Only As Strong As Its Foundation"

When digging a foundation, it requires that the workers climb down into a trench and work their way upward. The foundation of agape love in a relationship does not allow one partner to stand on the surface of the foundation and yell instructions down to the other partner. Agape love works together with cheerfulness and a willing heart seeking to share the burdens together.

"A building is only as strong as its foundation." A strong foundation provides the basis for building a relationship. Laborers begin building by digging down deep into the earth. They locate a stable area before they start pouring materials necessary to build the foundation. When a couple chooses to build on the surface, without deep probing, outside elements can cause the destruction of the relationship. It's not enough to just "have love;" love will be put to the test, and it must be solid enough to pass this test. Laboring together will sometimes bring hurt, misunderstandings, and tears. It's not enough to just "feel loved;" you must know you are loved and must convey to your partner that he or she is loved. I'm reminded of an old Bible school song; " And they'll know we are Christians by our love."

Building a foundation for marriage takes time. Just as a physical foundation needs time to settle, so does an intimate foundation. When Beverly and I purchased a new home, the house was beautiful and we were excited about its newness. However, there were times when we would hear creaking noises that sounded strange, after all it was a new home and everything should have been perfect. We discovered that the noises were from the new foundation settling into place. It wasn't enough that the cement was poured and had hardened. It needed to work itself into the depth of the earth. The foundation of new relationships also takes time to settle. Let me warn you that there is no established time limit or constraints. During the settling stage couples may hear and experience strange attitudes, hurt feelings, misunderstandings and other personality clashes that can make a couple think their relationship is no longer new. Men may began to wonder why their wife wants them to stop settling for the boys and now settle for her. Wives began to realize that they have to adjust to settling into a role that may be difficult in adapting. But I encourage you to keep strengthening yourselves, and your relationship will eventually settle into a solid foundation of understanding.

"Whosoever cometh to me, and heareth my saying, and doeth them, I will show you to whom he is like: He is like a man who built an house, and dug deep, and laid the foundation on a rock; and when a flood arose, the stream beat vehemently upon the house, and could not shake it; for it was founded upon a rock. But he that heareth, and doeth not, is like a man that, without a foundation, built an house upon the earth, against which stream did beat vehemently, and immediately it fell; and the ruin of that house was great" Luke 7: 47–49.

In this passage of scripture, Jesus provides three guidelines that believers should take into consideration when establishing a foundation: (1) Acknowledge Him, (2) Hear Him, (3) Follow His instructions. If you put these three principles into your relationship, you will have found the Rock in which to build upon, and that Rock is Jesus.

How many have gone before the throne, prayed, and asked Jesus, "Lord, is this the man or woman for me?" Most Christians have no problems with asking. It's the hearing and the following of the instructions that become the problem. And if you have to go to the altar of Jesus alone without your partner, this is a red flag. If God sent you this partner, you will connect and seek God's will for your lives together.

Many singles will ask, "How do I know When God sends me my partner?" My response is always " does that person treat you with the respect that God has for you?" God won't send you someone to force you to do something that is against His will.

It's important to search for an understanding of each other, to ask questions, and to gain insight when laying the foundation. I've counseled couples who have no knowledge about each other. They've never taken the time to just talk because they are too busy trying to impress or to cover-up an unholy mess. There were questions that needed to be asked, expectations that needed to be discussed, and assumptions that needed correcting. But they are now married and feel empty because they have no solid knowledge about each other to build upon. Such a couple has to build a marriage based on trail and error.

Some Are Afraid to Ask Questions Simply Because "They Can't Handle the Truth"

The reason why important questions are not asked from the beginning is a fear of intimidation. This reminds me of the motion picture "A Few Good Men" in which Jack Nicholson portrays an officer in the army, who is being questioned by Tom Cruise, who portrays a lawyer. The lawyer presses Jack Nicholson to tell the truth about an army cover-up, and he responds with, "You can't handle the truth". That's the reason why so many couples fail to ask important questions. They can't handle the truth. They are afraid that their partner may leave them for someone else. They know the truth but refuse to accept it. They would rather deal with the circumstances than the truth. However, is paying the price for the circumstances a greater cost than accepting the truth from the beginning?

I recently asked several individuals the questions they would ask if they were to remarry. Here are some answers:

"How often do you drink alcohol?"

"Is there a history of mental illness in the family?"

"How many other children do you have?"

"What caused your previous break-up, and what was your part?"

"What's our plan for disciplining your children?"

"Who's going to support your family after we've married?"

"When was the last time your had a medical physical?"

"What do you know about Christianity?"

"What is your relationship with your family?"

(Additional questions in appendix)

Don't be afraid to ask questions, and don't be afraid to face the facts even if they are negative. These facts don't mean that your relationship will end they just mean that you need to take time to resolve important issues.

Many think that true love conquers all. But true love should not have to conquer an issue that cannot be conquered. You may resolve to live with the issue, but this puts unnecessary pressure on the other factors involved in building the home of intimacy. You had the opportunity from the beginning to do better. However, you gave up hoping for what you wanted. You recognized that the foundation was going to be shaky, but you decided to play it by your ear, not God's.

I've been playing the piano for several years. When I was learning how to play, my parents would make me practice until a knew a song by "heart." I found out that meant that I was to study the song from the inside out, not just know it by ear, but study it until it reached my soul. Once it reached my soul, the other parts of my body would follow. It meant that my soul would relate the necessary style and pace to my fingers (staccato, or pianissimo), my facial expression would show confidence in my ability, my body would move with the grace of the music, and my feet would feel the rhythm and respond with a soft tapping. Because of what was in my soul, my whole body could relate and respond.

To Play by Ear Is Predicated on What Is Heard, Not What Is Known

There are times, however when I try to bypass the practice and try to play a song by ear. Playing by ear means I have to depend on what I hear, not what I know about the music. To play by ear is predicated on what is heard, not what is known. I could at any time during the song, lose my focus, stumble over chords, or not play to the fullest, often missing essential elements of the song. And it can get worse if I have to follow a soloist that I've never practiced with.

Take Time to Study Your Partner by Heart, Then You'll Understand That T.L.C. Is the Key to Understanding All Intimate Mysteries

As in music, your partner should be studied to the fullest and learned by heart. When you learn your partner by heart, you'll have the ability to recognize timing (when to talk or keep silent), you'll know your partner's style (when a no really means "yes"), and you'll know how, and when to approach certain issues at the appropriate time. When your heart is there, your mind and physical actions will respond with your partner's in intimate harmony.

When you play a relationship by ear, you never know what to expect from each other day to day. You're unsure of attitudes, feelings, or reactions. A relationship that continues on the surface never gains the ability to have a full knowledge of the other. And it's at that time when you began to fully understand the nature of Agape Love. Men will gain insight into why, during a certain time of the month, he has to walk on eggshells. Women won't be so perplexed when they've spent 15 minutes explaining something that they feel is important and their partner turns around and responds "Huh?, what'd you say?" He'll understand how to answer open-ended questions such as: "Do you think I'm gaining weight?", or "Does this outfit look good on me?" She'll have more patience when he constantly forgets to put the toilet seat down.

Playing by ear or faking often produces sour notes and sounds that are hurtful to the ears. Once a sour note is released into the sound waves, it can't be retrieved. What's worse is that, no matter how well you've played the song, the hearer will somehow always remember that sour note. Many couples playing it by ear will make verbal negative comments due to a lack of foundation or understanding. After the statement has been made, "I'm sorry, I really didn't mean what I said" is offered. But the sour statement is out there, and you can't pull it back.

Words are a gift of God. Without careful consideration, the wrong ones can destroy any home of intimacy.

"It's Not What You Say, But How You Say It"

"Let no corrupt communication proceed out of your mouth, but that which is good to the use of edifying, that it may minister grace unto the hearers" Ephesians 4: 29.

This scripture encourages that words were designed to edify. In a agape relationship, one thinks before he or she speaks. During counseling, I see couples who have to have the last word. "If you hurt me with a word, I'll find a harsher word or statement to hurt back." This is why Agape is so important. A relationship based on emotions only without a spiritual foundation, will inevitably want to fight back with harsh words instead of praying to find uplifting, edifying words. However, edification does not always mean verbally uplifting the other person. Silence also can edify. Every time you verbally fight back, you lose the battle of edification. Edifying often means to simply keep silent rather than rushing into a verbal ambush.

A Man Who Fights With Wife, Gets No Peace/Piece at Night

Agape love requires an exceptional amount of digging below the surface. To build a solid foundation, both partners must get down into the trench and dig. There's no room for friends, in-laws, church associates, co-workers, neighbors, or any other outside sources, except those involved in the building process. If you choose to invite their assistance, that's a choice that is made between both of you. But no one else has the right to assert authority in your building process. Many relationships have too many bosses and laborers involved in the building plans. During the foundation stage, it requires only the partners involved. My father told me that, when he met my mother and took her out the first time, my grandmother said to my mother, "If I were you, I wouldn't go anywhere with him. My father responded, "That's good, because I didn't come to take you out anyway." From that point on, my father had respect from her family who thought very highly of my father. They never had any problems with them interfering in their relationship even after they were married. They have been married for 40 years.

Establishing agape love requires many materials for marital stability:

action	Involvement	giving
purity	patience	total acceptance
support	commitment	edification
unconditional Love	sincerity	honesty
respect	sacrifice	behavior of well being

Below are 10 steps for incorporating the agape building materials into a foundation of intimacy:

1. Recognize who your partner is through his or her eyes, not yours!
2. Give the same measure of love that you expect in return.
3. Understand that each day will bring unexpected challenges, but Agape love will help you through.
4. Agape love will prevail when evil forces seek to overtake your relationship.
5. Agape love means pleasing your partner, whether or not he or she desires it.
6. Agape love will look beyond faults and recognize the needs of your partner.
7. Agape seeks to forget what your partner was in the past, but focuses on the present and future with hope and compassion.
8. Agape love is blind to societal standards unrelated to that of God's.
9. Agape love sets no time limits or boundaries on your relationship.
10. Agape love doesn't seek to jeopardize morals, standards, or values.

Chapter Fifteen

Constructing a Frame of Friendship Stability (Phileo Love)

"*For we are God's fellow workers; you are God's field, God's building. According to the grace of God which was given to me as a wise master builder I laid a foundation, and another is building upon it. But let each man be careful how he builds upon it.*" *I Corinthians 3: 9–10*

Phileo love is a verb derived from the Greek New Testament; it means to cherish and forsake all others. With Phileo love, you have a deep personal affection for your partner unlike that which anyone else can provide or give. When two people in marriage share themselves with each other, they develop Phileo love, with mutual affection, rapport, and friendship. They enjoy each other's company, laugh, and share fond moments whether they be good or bad. A Phileo love between a couple allows them to sit across from each other and smile with satisfaction about their relationship. Phileo love is an inner peace and is shown through total satisfaction with your partner.

Just because you are in a relationship does not mean that you are automatically best friends. Becoming best friends requires exchanging, as well as even accepting and rejecting the other's attitudes and behaviors.

When laborers frame a house, they connect the lumber together in various sizes, lengths, and shapes. The common material is the wood, supplied by the lumber company, but the laborers have to saw and design the wood to create the structure. God has given both men and women the ability to possess the "wood" of their relationship: their different thoughts, ideas, and characteristics. Once they have decided to come together in a relationship, it is their responsibility to patiently connect their personalities together to enhance their relationship. God has given us the material, the tools, and the instructions. It is the couple's job, as laborers working together, to carefully put the pieces together. A couple should work at becoming best friends from the beginning, and gradually be drawn closer together sharing common interests.

I love my wife especially because she was my friend first. We met at church on Sundays and saw each other at choir rehearsal on Thursdays. It's interesting that we had verbal contact, joking and engaging in other fun activities. But little did I know that our friendship would blossom into a marital relationship. I am proud to say that my wife is still my friend. She is caring, warm, sensitive and faithful. And most of all, she encourages me to be a strong family leader and continually lifts me up in prayer. And we are still growing in friendship as a married couple. It can be a struggle when two people who have been single and independent for so long, now having to live together with another person. Learning different habits, likes and dislikes. But I'm happy to say that through prayer and God's guidance, He is carefully constructing our personalities together on a daily basis. Not only for our good, but also for His good.   *Roy*

There Is Good Use in Everything,
If You Put Everything to Good Use

As Roy explains in his testimony, putting the pieces together as a couple requires diligence and sacrificial giving. Just as individuals are different, so are their needs. There have been times when individuals have met their partner, and have later found their relationship to be unequally balanced in personality material. If you meet a partner who does not possess the intimate personality that is capable of fulfilling your needs, it's the same as trying to fit a piece of lumber in a physical frame that has been incorrectly measured from the beginning. It is interesting to view couples that experienced conflicting issues from the time they met, but continued to carry the same issues into a marriage. They are now living in the same household and puzzled as to why they are not on one accord. However, they ignored the personality differences and tried to force them together into the frame anyway, without taking time to measure them. I've found that individuals will first match themselves together based on how they appear outwardly. Then, they will try to force their inward personalities together to balance their outward desire. And sometimes this situation does not always balance.

When laborers are building a home, they have to measure and carefully put the pieces together. If they are careless in their measurement, the materials will not fit properly into the frame. When constructing a frame of Phileo love, individuals must take the time to properly measure their partners' personality material so it can fit properly into the frame. In every relationship there are certain limitations and boundaries which should be recognized and respected. Without the proper measurements, a relationship will incorporate material that doesn't fit into the relationship.

From whom the whole body, being fitting and held together by that which every joint supplies, according to the proper working of each individual part,

causes the growth of the body for the building up of itself in love"
Ephesians 4: 16.

Paul makes emphasis that the marital body is fitted and joined together to produce one flesh. Each part of the body works together and provides a measure of support for the other parts which works toward edifying itself in love. When your partner reaches out to you for whatever reason, you need to provide support without thought of yourself. As one flesh, when your partner is hurt, you are hurt. When your partner is happy, you share in the happiness. The proper measurement of our contributing materials work to edify our relationship which, in turns assists in providing strength for your frame of phileo love.

What does it mean to become a best friend to your partner? Does it mean that he has to enjoy shopping with her or that she has to watch a sporting event without knowing the difference between a home run and a touchdown? How can two people become best friends if they don't have many things in common? The answer is that it is not that you have little in common, but you have failed to turn what you have in common into something. There is good use in everything, if you put everything to good use.

If you involve yourself in an activity and choose to ignore your partner, that activity does nothing toward building your relationship frame to make it stronger. There is a couple with whom I play golf. The husband tends to play a better game than his wife and is able to move along faster through the course. He has shared with me that the importance of the game to him was not winning or even competing, but spending the time with his wife. It's wonderful to observe these two people just enjoying each other's company in the beauty of nature without a need to rush. There are times when the husband will play a competitive game with other men, but the world stops when his wife steps on the course. There are activities that each individual needs for his or her own self-fulfillment, but personal activities should never dominate your relationship. Becoming best friends requires sharing, patience, and sacrifice. However, it is well worth it for the rewards you reap. And, it should also be mentioned that sex is not the only activity that a couple can engage in together. Your partner should be given just as much attention and energy outside of the bedroom as inside.

Becoming best friends requires that you both gain an understanding of each other without smothering the other. Some women may not understand that a man needs to spend some time around other men, just to enjoy the camaraderie, and male bonding. Men need to understand that women need the freedom to spend time with their women friends. Without such understanding, the relationship will feel smothering. However, relationships outside of the marriage should always be kept in the proper perspective.

A housewife who spends most of her time caring for her home and children, without any time for herself, will eventually feel unappreciated and used. A man who works diligently and supports his family, without having some personal time, will eventually develop stress. A phileo relationship will recognize this need for personal time and seek to fulfill this need. However, it is not Phileo love if it causes conflict in your relationship. Beverly and I are best friends, but I know that there are times when she needs to see her sisters and spend time talking and sharing with them. Because of their relationship, they fulfill a part of her that I cannot. A strong Phileo relationship cannot be built with selfishness or insecurity.

I was out to dinner one evening with some male friends. I happened to meet relatives dining at the same restaurant and went over to speak to them. After exchanging the customary "hellos," the wife, who has never said much to me since the day they were married, looked sternly at me and asked, "So, where's your wife?" I responded, "She's at home and I'm dining out with some friends." "You're not suppose to be out anywhere without your wife." I again responded, "It's okay. We've discussed it. It's not a problem, we've had dinner together at home, and I'm out with the guys having dessert and just talking." "Well, you should be home with your wife and not out with them!" What my relative's wife couldn't understand was that our relationship as best friends exists even when we are apart. Insecurity and jealousy will destroy the friendship frame of a relationship.

A couple consists of two human beings who become best friends through phileo love, by carefully putting the pieces together. Sometimes the pieces of your personalities will not automatically fit together. A relationship is comprised of Phileo love when the couple sits down together and evaluates what pieces of the personality fit and how the others that don't fit can be made to fit. Problems occur when a couple refuses to take the time to discern those personality pieces that need attention. A sturdy frame requires a couple putting together their strengths and working together to overcome their weaknesses. A strong phileo relationship requires that the couple look within themselves to determine their best material, and to give it to the other.

A Sturdy Phileo Frame Requires Three Principles

Forsaking All Others
Evaluating Personal Building Materials
Discarding Useless Material

…And Forsaking All Others

…And forsaking all others…And forsaking all others…And forsaking all others. Get the picture? I have heard this portion of the wedding vow being given priority with strict emphasis during a ceremony. The couple needs to understand that they are no longer two, but one flesh, and it is impossible to be one flesh with others involved. Forsaking all others only means making your partner a priority. Husband's and wives's must work together to cultivate their relationship. There may be times when one partner feels that the relationship is not growing and may want to kill it and start over. When I moved to my new house, there was a lemon tree in the garden. During the first several months, the tree appeared as if it was not going to grow or produce fruit; the leaves looked dry and lifeless. It was an eye sore, and I wanted to cut it down. My father heard my intent and shouted, "Son leave that tree alone. It only needs some love and attention." He suggested that I spend time watering and spreading plant food and, above all, have patience. I did as my father suggested, and later that year, the tree produced more lemons than we could handle. There are couples who have felt the the same about their relationship. If I had cut that tree down, I would have missed out on a fruitful blessing. Some couples have prematurely cut their relationship down without even taking the time to nurture it with prayer, kindness, love and most of all, patience.

Learning to forsake others can be emotionally straining, particularly when one has to phase out those who have been a part of your life for many years, contributing, encouraging, and guiding. There are times when family and friends make the marital requirement of "leaving and cleaving difficult."

God gives the instruction for a man to leave his father and mother and to cleave unto his wife, and they shall be one flesh (Genesis 2: 24). To cleave means to "stick" as with glue so that you can't be torn apart.

> When I first got married, I thought my husband would always be my friend. It was my impression that he would always be there for me when I needed him. After being married for two years, I've felt he has abandoned me as a friend. My feelings really don't take priority in his life. He seems to be best friends with his family and even his son's mother, while I have to wait until my turn comes. I really need him to be more sensitive to my feelings and pay more attention to my thoughts. I'm tired of being left out of his life and put at the bottom of the list. I married him for a lifetime companion, but somehow I still feel alone.   *Terri*

Terri's relationship lacks Phileo love which is the state of a couple being best friends through communication and the sharing of interests. Phileo love is being best friends, and best friends in a marriage means someone to talk with, someone who is available, someone who makes their partner a priority, and someone who provides protection.

A forsaking of all others can create jealously between those inside and outside of the relationship, as described by Terri, and can often lead to dissension in families and friendships. It was God's desire that the husband and wife depend on each other, not parents or friends, for any support whether emotional or financial. Forsaking does not mean closing the door on all friends and associates, but simply making your partner a priority. If your relationship has not gained the strength to forsake all others, there will be problems in your friendship frame. If every time there is a disagreement and one partner has to involve other sources for support, the frame is not sturdy. It is important that couples spend time solving their own issues within their home of intimacy.

"They're Afraid of Being Labeled "Hen Pecked."

Early in our relationship one of my wife's sisters would question her whenever I was out with my male friends. "Aren't you afraid he's out doing something wrong?" " Do you really trust him?" The problem was that my sister-in-law had relationships with unfaithful men. In her mind, no man could be trusted. However, Beverly was confident that our relationship was strong, and there was no reason to think otherwise. Our relationship is based on trust. I always tell couples that, when in doubt, they should talk to their partner. However, many men have a problem with this. They're afraid of being labeled "hen pecked," or seen as "reporting in," based on the old standard of "who is wearing the pants in the family" and "who is the king of the castle." Even women have to defend themselves against such comments as, "I thought you had that man wrapped around your finger" or "Did you marry your daddy?" You weren't stupid enough to leave that "to obey" statement in your vows, were you?" All these negative attacks give couples the impression that they must defend their commitment to forsake all others. "It shouldn't matter to anyone else who wears the pants in your relationship if they are not the one washing them." In laws, relatives, best friends take a back seat to your relationship, and they should stay there unless invited to the front. And you must be very careful who you invite into the front seat; they may be eventually driving off with your partner while you now stand by the side of the road. However, couples have an obligation to each other to serve and satisfy without validation from anyone but God.

"It Should Not Matter to Anyone Else Who Wears the Pants in Your Relationship."

Evaluating & Constructing Personal Building Materials

A frame of Phileo love means taking the time to evaluate those things within your personality that can be brought to your marriage to build a friendship of strength. God has created each individual with a distinctive personality. When two different personalities come together, there will be a difference of opinions. Remember, to evaluate personality materials that will be effective, not only in the present, but also in the future of your relationship. Take into consideration those little habits that you may think are cute in the beginning but may become annoying as the relationship progresses.

When I was in college, I lived with three other guys from three different backgrounds and personalities. We were good friends prior to moving in together. However, once together in an enclosed place, our friendship faced many challenges. Each man had his own basic living standards and, to peaceable live together, we had to evaluate each individual personality and work together accordingly. One roommate would spend a long time in the bathroom most mornings, another would get upset if anyone read the paper before he did, and I felt that the kitchen and dishes should be cleaned after every meal. We survived, but it took a lot of time and understanding. This illustrates why it is so important to spend quality time with your partner to evaluate Phileo building material. Spending quality time means the television is off, the answering machine is on, children properly placed, and you allow nothing to interfere with your time. Building a home of intimacy needs to be built with those characteristics that exist between you as a couple. A man should not expect his wife to have the same personality as his mother, nor should a wife expect her husband to have the same personality as her father. The purpose of constructing a frame is to be able to live with whom you have chosen to marry so you can share the attitudes, feelings, and characteristics that brought you together. It means looking within the heart of yourself and your partner and viewing those things which will become an asset to the frame.

The evaluative phase of building usually takes place when we are at our best. Hours are spent preparing for your partner in the beginning of the relationship. There is impressive language, best manners, leaving a lasting memory of happiness. There should be a feeling within the spirit that leads insight into your partner's personality and characteristics, regardless of how they appear on the outside. The problem occurs when the spiritual insight is ignored. The blueprints of 1 Peter 3: 1–9 describes how to evaluate what personality is needed when building a sturdy frame of phileo friendship. So many couples suffer with this lack of understanding when evaluating their partner for friendship. The basis of the scripture gives couples the information needed to live peacefully within their home as one flesh. And at the same time receive blessings from God in the relationship.

To fully evaluate material for the phileo frame, partners should be seen as they really are, without the nice clothes, the make-up, and other outwardly pleasing appearances. When a developer decides to build a track of new homes, he first builds model homes for perspective buyers to view. The model homes are filled with plush carpeting, exquisite decorations, beautiful furniture, and each room is decorated to give a feeling of a warm home. Often, buyers get caught up in the beauty of the models and forget that the finished product will not be as elaborately decorated, and they must do so themselves. Individuals are often deceived by partners in this way. What is seen on the outside is often different from what we have to work with on the inside. Many Phileo frames have come together and have eventually fallen apart because it was made of "imitation materials". God developed the institution of marriage and modeled it through the relationship between Jesus Christ and the church.

Once you've taken quality time to evaluate the materials used for building your home of intimacy, you can begin the process of patiently constructing the materials together to form a solid relationship. Unlike prefabricated homes in which the lumber is cut, the materials are supplied, and there are instructions on how to put the pieces together, the couple is on their own. However, good relationships don't come ready made or prefabricated as some physical homes; individuals are different and so are relationships needs. To build a lasting and fulfilling relationship, personality differences will have to be made to fit.

To build a frame of Phileo love, a couple needs to work together in faith and trust that God will guide them in building their personalities and becoming true witnesses of His blessings. One of your Christian witnesses is that of your relationship. If your relationship is not spiritually enhancing, your witness is a failure and lacks biblical support. However, if your relationship is established and true Phileo love exists, God will get the glory and others witnessing your relationship will view it as true holy matrimony.

PUTTING THE FRAME TOGETHER:

"The beginning of wisdom is: Acquire wisdom; And with all your acquiring, get understanding" Proverbs 4: 7.

Does your relationship frame need more understanding? Are there personality materials that you both have not explored between each other because you have not taken the time to inquire? The more you inquire, the more you will acquire an understanding about your partner's personality, and their benefits. Below is a partial list of personality materials that can strengthen any relationship frame. List those personality skills that you as a couple possess and those that can be added that will develop your Phileo friendship frame. Remember, the frame is composed of material that is based on inward appearance, not necessarily outward appearance.

artistic	inventive	determined	organizer	comforting
loyal	witty	curious	friendly	strong
tolerant	encouraging	clever	neat	open-minded
persistent	cooperative	joyful	planner	giving
settled	self-directed	respected	individualistic	perfectionist
persuasive	talented	thrifty	active	sociable
outgoing	reserve	forceful	capable	growing
progressive	courageous	graceful	self-aware	eager
considerate	ambitious	trustworthy	goal-directed	forgiving
self-reliant	understanding	disciplined	nurturing	expressive

Discarding Useless Material

"But, I say, walk by the spirit, and you will not carry out the desires of the flesh. Now the deeds of the flesh are evident, which are: immorality, impurity, sensuality, idolatry, sorcery, enmities, strife, jealousy, outbursts of anger, disputes, dissensions, factions, envying, drunkenness, carousing, and things like these, of which I forewarned you just as I have forwarded you that those who practice such things shall not inherit the kingdom of God" Galations 5: 16; 19–21

In every construction sight, there is a pile of junk that the laborers have thrown to the side. In that pile there's left over lumber, rocks, trash, and other debris that were found to be useless to the structure. After a couple thoroughly evaluates personal building material and carefully attempts to put chosen pieces together, there is the task of throwing away unnecessary materials that you as a couple have found to be useless. The important question is "What do we throw away?" The answer is simple. You throw away those materials that serve no purpose in the building of your home of intimacy. This is why it is important to be led by the Spirit and not by the flesh. For example, a couple determines that their relationship needs sensitivity in the frame of friendship. Then, insensitivity should be placed into the discard pile.

One Father's Day, I was in my office preparing materials for an upcoming seminar. My mind was focused on gathering information and creating an outline. My children ran into my office, excited and yelling, "Happy Father's Day," and presented me with a gift. I stopped my work and opened the box, Beverly came into the office and asked if I liked the gift. I was happy and responded with a smile since I had told them they did not have to buy me anything. I said "Thank You," and went back to work. Later that evening, I sensed that Beverly had a different attitude, and I asked if something was wrong. She stated that I had hurt her feelings earlier. I asked her what I did. She told me that when I was presented with my gift, it appeared that I didn't like it because of my lack of enthusiasm. My attention was focused on my work and instead of taking a few moments to exchange hugs and kisses with my children, I just went back to work. I apologized for my insensitivity and expressed my appreciation for her sharing how she felt and not just holding a grudge. Because we talked right away, we could move on with our relationship. The attitude I had on Father's Day went into the discard pile and that type of incident will never happen again. As a relationship grows, the desire should be to build up the positive and discard the negative. Negativity weakens a frame of Phileo friendship. Similarly, when a home is built with termite infested wood, the termites will eventually destroy the frame. If an internal negative feeling continues, it can manifest itself outwardly and damage a relationship.

Evil thoughts, damaging words, and other unedifying behavior should be thrown into the discard pile. The discard pile should include those things that do not promote happiness between a couple. Building a frame of Phileo love means working together and agreeing not to hold grudges or to intentionally hurt your partner. Discarding unnecessary material means that partners do not keep personal ammunition available in the case of disagreements. When one partner is verbally offended, the first impulse is to respond with a more damaging verbal assault. It's similar to "shooting from the hip", the quickest partner to the draw with the most damaging information. In most cases the verbal assaults are filled with past circumstances that brought hurt to the relationship. Thus, past hurts should be thrown into the discard pile and left there forever. Discarding the negative leaves more room for the positive, and promotes a sturdy home of intimacy.

TIME TO THROW IT AWAY:

"To sum it up, let all be harmonious, sympathetic, brotherly, kind-hearted, and humble in spirit; not returning evil for evil, or insult for insult, but giving a blessing instead; for you were called for the very purpose that you might inherit a blessing" 1 Peter 3: 8–9

There are things that enhance the growth of a relationship, and others that prevent growth. This project requires that a couple come together and search their relationship for useless materials that prevent optimum growth. Below is a partial list of personality materials that can cause a relationship frame to be built with problem infested material. Take time to evaluate your personality frame in order to prevent any further infestation of internal damage. Use this opportunity to free your mind, and at the same time, free your soul.

jealousy	neglect	disrespect	dishonor
selfishness	pride	negativity	condescending
revengeful	abusive	unsupportive	resistant
ridiculing	thrifty	frivolous	frightening

Chapter Sixteen
Intimately Decorating (Eros Love)

"*Let the husband render to his wife the affection due her, and likewise also the wife to her husband. Do not deprive one another except with consent for a time...and come together again so that Satan does not tempt your because of your lack of self-control.*" 1 Corinthians 7: 3,5

Now comes the exciting part of the building process; creatively decorating your home of intimacy. In a loving partnership, enjoying sexuality and connecting with a partner are decorations each brings to the other willingly, not by demands or coercion. When a physical home is built, the foundation, frame, and exterior construction have to be built based on the specifications of the blueprints. Once completed it becomes the responsibility of the couple to decorate the inside of the home based on their own personal taste and enjoyment. Decorating intimately can be described as any activity that adds intimate beauty to your relationship. To intimately decorate means that you seek to do those things that bring happiness and cheer to your relationship. It must be understood that intimately decorating does not always mean engaging in sexual activity. One partner can intimately decorate with the other by spending more quality time or by shopping and buying the other a surprise gift. Intimate decorating can be further described as any activity that a couple finds pleasurable together. Intimately decorating becomes special because of the effort involved. I have heard women comment that their husband may not be a great cook, but their intimate fulfillment is through the effort and time he took to create the meal.

A well developed and decorated relationship can provide a sense of internal comfort that a physical action can only introduce and an internal action can establish. An intimately decorated couple can be described as those that compliment each other, the wife makes the husband looks good and vise-versa. I'm reminded of a church that presented their Pastor and wife an anniversary celebration. The Pastor had only been married to his wife for about one year. Some of the members were asked to give congratulatory comments, and it was interesting to hear each member speak well about the Pastor's new wife. Their comments signified how the Pastors attitude was different, he appeared to be happier and some even commented that he even preached with greater enthusiasm. Based on these comments, this couple had intimately decorated each other with inner love and it shone through their outward affection, and was felt by others.

There Is True Intimacy in Christianity

Beverly and I went on a cruise with the married couple's ministry from our church. It was a precious gift to witness 14 married couples "dating" and falling in love all over again. They sat at the dinner table, whispering, giggling, and cuddling, taking moonlit strolls on the top deck of the ship and dancing cheek to cheek to romantic music. One couple decided to wrap up in a blanket and star gaze. These intimate activities they participated in at sea were activities they had never considered doing at home. The reason they were able to be so romantic on this cruise was that they had no other place to go. There were no phone calls, demanding children, housework, or other distractions. The only thing they had to do was to renew their intimate relationship. It gave each couple an opportunity to come together again as one flesh, sharing emotional and physical intimacy, fulfilling the desires of the heart and soul. The most wonderful part was that, even though there were others absorbed in a variety of secular activities, as a group we were still able to maintain our Christian witness and to demonstrate that there is intimacy in Christianity.

It Was a Precious Gift to Witness 14 Married Couples Dating and Falling in Love All Over Again

To become one flesh requires that a couple spend time gradually learning each other in every aspect of the biblical term "to *know.*"...."Adam *knew* Eve his wife, and she conceived" Genesis 4: 1. How much do you really *know* your partner?

The union includes more than just the physical, and this is without shame between marital partners. Shame in martial sex was never imparted by God. Instead, the biblical expression for sexual intercourse between husband and wife is to know, an expression of profound dignity. Physical intimacy is nothing that should cause shame. It is something that God has provided between husband and wife as an activity of special joy, that is different than any other activity. Eros love is a physical exchanging of intimate feelings and thoughts, as well as fantasies.

My problem with intimacy stems back to a childhood of loneliness, having no father, no siblings and no one to really "connect" with. I believe my lack of connection with my family left me feeling awkward in my marriage. For myself, not having that interaction or close bond with any male figure, it left me feeling fearful and shy when it came to intimate relationships. For this reason, I believe, I married a very passive, emotionally unavailable man. I felt very comfortable and safe with him. However, I also felt very lonely. And because that feeling of a lack of emotional intimacy is such an uncomfortable place to be, I would allow myself to be around individuals who were uncaring and sometimes even mean—as long as I was getting that attention and having at least some kind of inter-action or connection ,even though it was a negative one. Robin

Couples will enter into marriage with the idea that the penis and vagina are the main focus of intimate fulfillment, and the two body parts come together and act independently, without involving other emotional factors. When they discover that there are no fireworks they become disappointed and turn away from each other. There are instances where individuals engage in sexual activity for the first time and, because of a bad experience, lose the desire for future activity. They do not always relate this loss of desire to his or her partner, who continues in the relationship not understanding that their partner is experiencing intimate difficulties. A sexual relationship is not necessarily self-fulfilling, but can become so if both partners accept responsibility. If a couple seeks to communicate sexual feelings without inhibitions and shame, they can work together to decorate their home of intimacy.

Boost Your Partner's Ego, Boost Your Partner's Libido

If there is no trust, then a partner will be reluctant in sharing intimate concerns for fear that he or she will be ignored or not taken seriously. With any marriage relationship, each partner has to be conscious and exercise sensitivity and consideration toward the other, paying attention to the other's reactions or feelings. If one partner notices or senses an uncomfortable or insecure feeling from the other, it should be his or her desire to assist in restoring personal confidence. It's at this time when couples should share their intimate feelings and desires in an effort to receive the pleasure they desire. However, a partner must also work indi-vidually within themselves to resolve such issues. A partner can help, of course, but the individual component must be attended to.

"Words of Intimacy That Give Men a Tone of Corniness, Give Women a Feeling of Horniness"

Understanding with sensitivity means you work with your partner, and if your partner has sensitivity, he or she will accept your feelings and work with you. Learn to boost your partner's ego, and at the same time, you will boost your partner's libido. To boost an ego and a libido means to sensuously communicate your feelings through tone of voice and physical movement during intercourse. If your partner's sexual technique is rough and uncomfortable, speak in a soft sensuous voice relating how he or she can be more tender and use your hands to direct the proper motion that will cause pleasure. It's important to realize that when you both are satisfied, you are both happy. Encourage your thoughts, encourage your partner's heart. Some men are afraid to share intimate feelings for fear of sounding "corny." However, "words of intimacy that give men a tone of corniness, give women a feeling of horniness." Simply having a conversation expressing your partner's beauty from head to toe and the feelings that you receive from focusing on your partner's body can go a long way toward achieving sexual pleasure. Don't be afraid to tell each other, there will always be a level of fear in every relationship. The fear of women is engaging in sex without receiving satisfaction, and the fear of men is engaging in sex without giving satisfaction. With faithfulness toward each other and prayer for God's guidance, the fear can be turned into confidence. I know this sounds strange, praying to God for help with how to sexually satisfy your partner. Why not? He created you and your partner, and He knows what methods work best with your individual desires for intimacy.

The Fear of Women Is Engaging in Sex Without Receiving Satisfaction, and the Fear of Men Is Engaging in Sex Without Giving Satisfaction

As a human being, you don't know it all. This is evident because of the many relationships that continue day after day, year after year, unfulfilled. Too many couples are just occupying the space without taking time to dwell in the place. Just occupying the space means that one partner is simply satisfied with the fact that there is a relationship, that he or she has a companion. They are basically taking up space with their partner's life. They are not spending the quality time needed to decorate their relationship emotionally or physically. When this occurs it may be because the partner just does not know how to the dwell in the space. He or she does not realize what his or her partner needs and is afraid to admit that he or she is are not aware. For example, the wife is afraid that she will disappoint her husband if he discovers that she is not intimately satisfied, and her husband does not ask; just engages. Therefore, time after time, they occupy the space of a physically sexual couple, but do not take the time to dwell in the space of an intimately loving couple.

Too Many Couples are Just Occupying the Space Without Taking Time to Dwell in the Place

It can be of a great help to any sexual relationship if the couple understands that there is a physical sexual cycle that males and females encounter during sexual intercourse. Developing the skills needed to complete the cycle can provide intimate results. To engage in sex, but deny your partner the opportunity to complete his or her sexual cycle, is usually due to a lack of knowledge regarding the physiological nature of your partner, or the sex cycle, or even how to incorporate the cycle in your intimate relationship.

Sex Is More Than Just Putting a Penis and Vagina Together

The word *sex* is sometimes never used or discussed. When I first began teaching marriage enhancement techniques at my church, I felt it was important to teach the foundational biblical issues related to marriage. This meant that I had to teach sexual issues which included a presentation of male and female models of genital parts, and I had to instruct couples on enhancing their sexual techniques. One of the single female seniors within the church felt it was disrespectful and inappropriate to teach such a subject. Her argument was that "individuals know the parts God has given them, and they don't need no instruction on their use." True, men know they were born with a penis and women with a vagina. The problem comes when couples don't understand that fulfilling sex takes more than just putting a penis and vagina together. With this woman's attitude, she would be depriving these couples from gaining a full understanding of something that God created as wonderful.

Would it be better that these couples were taught marriage enhancement outside of the church, rather than within? God has gifted men and women with the equipment, but a couple needs to work together to enhance their use. In some cases, couples have not discovered the deeply beautiful decoration that God has given when he created man and woman. They simply stay on the surface and fear exploring the wonders of sex and intimacy. It's similar to having a full range of appliances within your home and not taking time to read the instructions. There was a time when my family would come home from church and have to wait to eat while the food warmed in the oven. It was two years later when I finally read the instructions completely regarding my stove and learned that the oven had a timer. The following Sunday, before leaving for church, I set the timer and put the food in the oven. Upon arriving home, there was this beautiful aroma that met us at the doorway; the food was hot and ready for serving. Just think, I could have saved my family the frustration of extended hunger if I would have only taken the time to explore the full benefits of that appliance. There are many couples involved in sexual relationships who are not receiving the full aroma of an intimate relationship. They settle for routine sexual activity, not taking the time to fully explore themselves or their partner. Couples spend many years unsatisfied with their sexual relationship and do nothing about it.

It Was Not God's Desire That an Intimate Relationship have Plain Walls or Empty Spaces

If a couple never takes time to decorate their home of intimacy, it will forever be empty. The interior decoration within our physical homes are filled with items that Beverly and I thought would enhance our home. Continuously looking at plain walls and empty rooms can bring depression and boredom. It was not God's plan that a relationship have plain walls or empty spaces. It was His desire that a man and woman decorate their intimate home with their intimacy. God asks that both partners wholeheartedly work together to please each other.

Within any relationship, there will be disagreements and disappointments when it comes time to decorate your relationship with intimacy. Both partners have their own desires, ideas, and fantasies. Without a level of maturity, knowledge, and understanding, the relationship will eventually suffer and become as a house with empty rooms and plain walls. Further, the longer a couple waits to decorate, the harder it is to gain the motivation. When partners enjoy intimately decorating themselves, they work hard not to allow anyone or any circumstance to come between their intimate relationship.

One barrier to intimacy that comes to mind is pregnancy. This period during a relationship can cause unexpected changes, from physical to emotional, and definitely sexual. There are many concerns whether intercourse will be uncomfortable, or what does he or she expect from the other? Pregnancy is a delicate time in a marriage and can have a lasting effect for good or ill on a couple's sexual and intimate adjustment within a relationship.

My husband and I have been married for 12 years and currently have six children, with another on the way. Learning to continue intimacy during my pregnancy required a conditioning of mental, spiritual, and physical preparation. I needed all three components to effectively please myself as well as my husband. I had to pray as an individual for the purpose of learning how to meet his needs, and he did the same. It was not that I did not want my husband intimately. Mentally, I had the desire, but physically my body just would not respond. Within me, I knew God wanted me to to be a submissive wife and satisfy my husband, but I needed for Him to give me the strength.

During these times, God has shown me not to avoid my husbands need for intimacy, but to involve him in every aspect of each pregnancy. We have found that by communicating our feelings, sharing our needs, we have become very creative in our intimate relationship. Through God's direction, we have found that intimacy is more than just sexual intercourse, but it is being able to edify each other mentally, which in turns increases my physical desire. We also discuss ways to compromise our intimacy, whereas he becomes sensitive to my condition and I become sensitive to his desires. We've learned alternative sexual positions and behavior, and have exercised our creative knowledge of each other's body. Pregnancy should never become a barrier to intimacy, but should be considered a period where a couple can spend quality time sharing in new changes and exploring other techniques of intimate fulfillment.   *Doreen*

When it comes time to intimately decorate, there are surprises, disappointments and barriers that will surface in various circumstances other than pregnancy. The "art of sex" has dominated the world with many expectations and a variety of erotic expressions and, as a result, many have problems separating reality from fantasy. After spending time counseling couples and conducting seminars in the area of sex and intimacy, the same statement always surfaces from the men, "She doesn't understand my needs," and from the women, "all he wants is sex and I feel used." The purpose of intimately decorating your relationship with Eros love is to fulfill the needs of both individuals.

Always remember that your relationship is between you and your partner and should never be compared to anyone or anything else. It cannot be compared because each individual and each relationship is different. It is the same as visiting the physical home of another couple, observing their furniture, and decor, and leaving disappointed with your personal physical home because it may not be furnished as nicely. To constantly compare it with others will only bring depression. Couples need to strive to intimately decorate their relationship for their own needs, without regard to what others do. The intimacy part of a relationship should be the most sacred and private moments between two partners who honestly share their physical, emotional, and sensual feelings without any inhibitions or fear that their partner will invite visitors into their intimate home.

A Sexual Relationship Between a Husband and Wife Should be Manifested Through an Inner Glow

There are times when it is wonderful to receive and even give decorating ideas, but never share the feelings of your partner with anyone. The sexual relationship between a husband and wife should stay within the interior of their home of intimacy, but the inner glow of satisfaction will be evident outwardly.

Creating the M.O.O.D
(The Love Making Cycle)

"I'm not in the mood." Does this sound familiar? It is a statement made by both men and women. To ultimately decorate a room requires a certain mood. The mood sets the feeling that the decorator wishes to convey about a room. Since my hobby is golf, the furniture and decoration in my study is composed of a golfing decor. So while I relax in my study, I experience a mood of being on the golf course. Our family room has a mood of relaxation and comfort, with an impression of family unity. And, of course, our bedroom, provides a feeling of privacy, security and intimacy. The door has a lock that we use without any reservation.

Women Have One Head, While Men Have Two Heads

Decorating intimately requires setting the right mood. When it comes to moods of intimacy as usual men and women differ. If a woman is upset, her mood is not one in which her husband should request intimacy. However, for a man, mood does not matter when it come to sex. This can be better understood if we realize that women have to work with only one head. In this one head, they have to focus on several needs all at the same time—children, work, and intimacy. If she is focusing on an issue other than intimacy, then her mood will suffer. However, men have two heads,—one for stress and one for sex. A man can think about other issues with the head on his shoulders, while engaging in sex with the head of his penis. This means that each partner must be mindful and carefully create the appropriate mood and the appropriate time to intimately decorate with sexual and intimate beauty. Setting the right mood is predicated on incorporating what I've detailed in the four steps for creating the M.O.O.D.: Motivation, Observation, Operation and Determination. Each step builds upon the other for the purpose of creating the right M.O.O.D. when intimately decorating your home of intimacy.

When the time comes to decorate a physical home, it is important to spend time concentrating on how each piece will look or what impression the decorator wants to make in a room. Choosing various themes, color schemes, and furniture all take time, but bring a room to life. A serious decorator spends countless hours trying to produce the right mood and effect. Mixing and matching, changing and spacing, a place for everything and everything in its place. Arousing the desire to intimately decorate a relationship requires that both partners recognize the personality of the other and arouses him or her accordingly. Whereas motivation for a man can be instantaneous, based on physical attraction, it takes a woman longer and requires a more creative act to produce full arousal, to complete the M.O.O.D. This may mean experimenting with various techniques, sexual positions, and searching for those pressure points that must be penetrated properly to obtain peak performance. Every person is born with erogenous zones. God designed our bodies so that our hormones, nerve endings, and minds can create sexual arousal. These are natural reactions, created by God, and as part of a married couple, they should be encouraged.

A Project of Exploration

Listed are female and male genital erogenous zones. As a project, spend several evenings, without interruptions, to fully explore these intimate areas of your partner. Feel free to explore them by using whatever means! USE YOUR IMAGINATION! The purpose is to become more acquainted with your partner's intimate decorations to better enhance your sexual experiences.

Female Genital Erogenous Zones

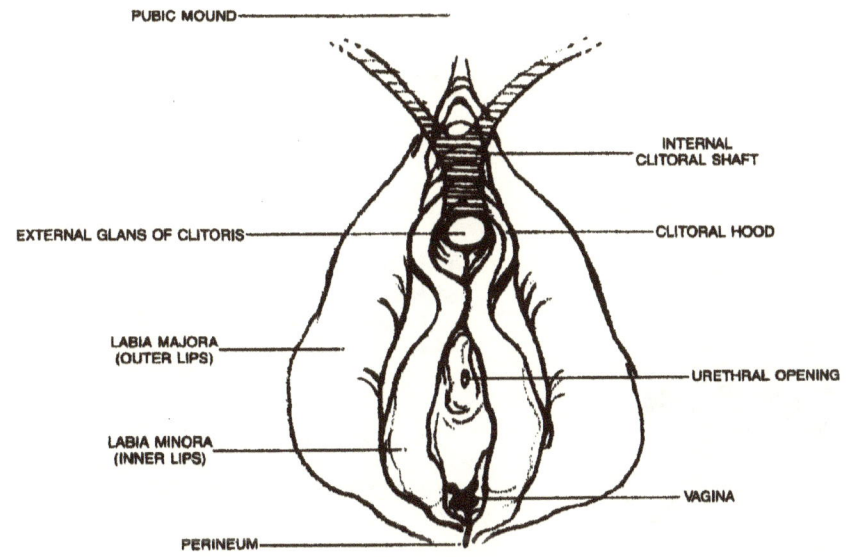

The *labia* are the outer and inner lips and have many nerve endings that create sexual excitement. Creative techniques should include gently touching this area to build sexual tension.

The *clitoris* is part of the external genitals of the female, situated at the anterior meeting of the labia minora and made up of two small erectile bodies, a glans and a hood. Clitoral stimulation requires careful consideration, attention, and coordination. The wife must first become aware of what kinds of stimulation arouse her and then instruct her husband to perform the correct stimulation.

The *vagina* is the canal in the female that receives the penis in copulation, existing as a potential space capable of contraction and expansion. This area can be stimulated through masturbation or penile stimulation.

Carefully creating stimulation through various techniques and sexual positions can create sensations leading to orgasm.

The *perineum* is the soft tissue between the vagina and the anus. This area is very sensitive and can be used to create sexual pleasure.

Male Genital Erogenous Zones

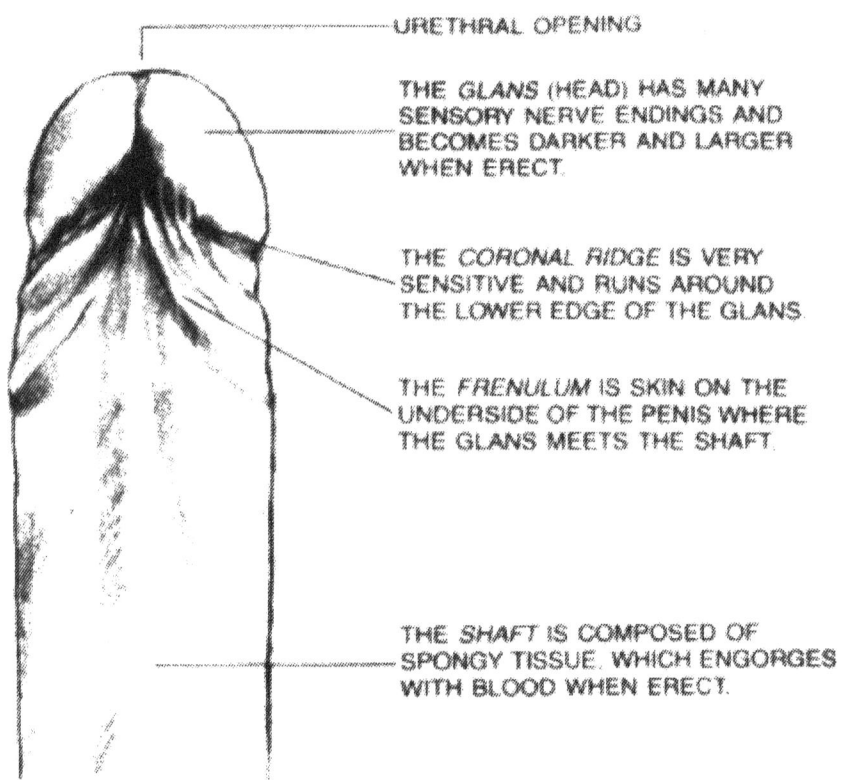

URETHRAL OPENING

THE GLANS (HEAD) HAS MANY SENSORY NERVE ENDINGS AND BECOMES DARKER AND LARGER WHEN ERECT.

THE *CORONAL RIDGE* IS VERY SENSITIVE AND RUNS AROUND THE LOWER EDGE OF THE GLANS.

THE *FRENULUM* IS SKIN ON THE UNDERSIDE OF THE PENIS WHERE THE GLANS MEETS THE SHAFT.

THE *SHAFT* IS COMPOSED OF SPONGY TISSUE, WHICH ENGORGES WITH BLOOD WHEN ERECT.

The *penis* is an external organ that consists primarily of spongy tissue bound in thick membrane sheaths. The penis requires a rapid stroking when producing orgasm. The head of the penis has sensitive nerve endings which can be stimulated through masturbation or vaginal stimulation. The husband needs to teach his wife how to stroke his penis to provide maximum pleasure.

The *scrotum and testicles* are the thin, loose sac of skin that contains the testes and has a layer of muscle fibers that contract involuntarily. The testicles are very sensitive if gently touched with soft fingers or even a tongue.

The *perineum* is the soft tissue between the scrotum and the anus. As with women, this area is very sensitive and can be used to create sexual pleasure.

Spend Time Searching for Those Tiny Crevices, and Neglected, Sensitive Spaces That Can Benefit from Intimate Attention

It is all right to touch and to respond to these intimate contacts described above, because it enhances your sensuality and develops a mutual desire for sex. I have a relative who is very gifted at interior decorating. It does not matter what size of room, type of furniture, or decorations it contains, she has the skill to bring a drab room to life. She is capable of moving the furniture, designing a proper place, and if it does not work to her eye, she has no problem with moving things around and trying a new look. As a couple works to decorate themselves intimately, they must also take time to vary their lovemaking without being afraid of exploring their partner's most intimate areas, searching for those tiny crevices, areas often neglected, and sensitive spaces that can bring about and benefit from intimate attention. It is important to take time to develop this skill and to bring these areas of your partner's body to life. Bringing it to life does not always mean sexual intercourse, but simply spending an evening exploring each other's needs.

The Beauty of the Songs of Solomon
Is the Sharing of Intimate Words

Just as God has provided designs for building a foundation of agape love, and constructing a frame of phileo friendship love, he also has provided designs for decorating a home of intimacy with Eros love. There is a specific section in God's blueprint that provides enlightenment on creating erotic love. The entire book of the Song of Solomon is a love story created through erotic symbolism and poetic imagery. The beauty of the book is the sharing of intimate thoughts and feelings between a bride and groom, an encounter filled with erotic preparation before the manifestation of sexual consummation. The bride and groom seek to decorate themselves with the physiological creation that God had given to them. Solomon and his bride were not ashamed in speaking of their erotic desire for each others love.

"A garden enclosed is my sister, my spouse; a spring shut up, a fountain sealed" Song of Solomon 4: 12. The garden refers to his bride's vagina, a place that is beautiful and filled with sexual refreshment. Notice that Solomon refers to his wife's genitals as a special place created especially for him. As men, there should be an understanding that women prefer terms of splendor when referring to their most intimate parts. To refer to her genitalia as something other than a wonderful and special place is insulting and degrading, not only to the created, but also to the Creator (God). The term "a spring shut-up" means that she is a virgin and no one has ever entered into her sexually. The rocks around it refers to it having been hidden and protected from strangers or intruders. The bride saved her special intimate decoration for her husband.

Motivation
(Arousal Phase)

"It makes me feel special when my wife initiates sex"

"I love when my husband rubs my feet softly and speaks sweetly"

"My greatest foreplay begins when my partner teases me before we go off to work and reinforces that feeling throughout the day with telephone calls."

"Timing is everything. I can become aroused when my partner guides me slowly, touching me and not neglecting any part of my body."

The motivation of M.O.O.D. is the arousal stage of a sexual relationship, which should begin with a thought of how to arouse your partner and prepare him or her for intimacy. Motivation for arousal means exercising practices that fit your partner's intimate needs. The arousal stage, which is often called foreplay, should not start at the moment of physical contact, but should begin hours and even days before. Due to the physiological nature of men, most arousal is instantaneous, based on visual observation. However, for women, arousal should be viewed as planting seed that needs watering to grow. Men are aroused by visual contact, women are aroused by mental contact. Until couples understand the difference, they will continue to struggle with the stage of motivation.

God's blueprint as expressed in the erotic dialogue between Solomon and his bride, intimately decorate each other using symbolic imagery to create a M.O.O.D. of erotic arousal. Solomon speaks of his bride's kisses being sweet, as though they were dripping with honey. *Thy lips, O my spouse, drop like the honeycomb; honey and milk are under thy tongue, and the scent of thy garments is like the fragrance of Lebanon" Song of Solomon 4: 11*. The interpretation of the honey and milk under her tongue has been interpreted as "French kissing." Since the tongue bears the sense of taste, for Solomon to comment about honey and milk under her tongue, his tongue must have explored that area and tasted sweetness. While there are some who think that "French kissing" is vulgar or unsanitary, between a husband and wife, it can be loving. Solomon continues to become aroused by his intimate partner, and he notices that she has decorated herself in a perfumed negligee. Dressing for sex is very important, especially for women. Solomon was immediately aroused at her sight. Remember, your husband is aroused by visual perception. To greet him with rollers, face cream, or an old gown or robe is not intimately arousing. A man can become aroused by the physical beauty of his partner, or even more when her body is decorated with his favorite style of lingerie. The sheerness of the garment presents a tantalizing partial view of his partner's body that adds desire. Sexy lingerie can be an erotic decoration for both males and females. And depending on the style and material of the garment, can accentuate physical features. The choice of color can help develop a romantic mood. Red represents hot passion, black represents sensuousness, purple or pink represents a warm, soft passion, and white represents purity or innocence.

For wives, this type of intimate preparation takes time and energy, which cannot be easily accomplished on a daily basis. With either children, work, or household responsibilities, I know that women may be exhausted at the end of the evening. You think, after all, my husband is going to remove all the decoration, anyway. My solution is directed toward the husbands. If it is your desire that your wife give you 100% in sex, give her 100% in all the rest. The less energy she exerts in everything else, the more energy she will have for sex.

If You Desire 100% During Sex, Give 100% in Everything Else

Where women should develop the skill of visual arousal, men should learn to develop the skill of arousing their wife through physical preparation also. Women appreciate their husbands taking the time to dress in erotic and enticing clothing and to be clean shaven and freshly bathed. In addition to this physical preparation, he can also arouse her with sensuous conversation. I can remember a woman asking, "Why is it that the woman has to spend time preparing herself for bed, and the man just comes to bed with holes in his socks, dirty underwear, and other visual unappealing attire?" My response was that where "men will sacrifice the intimate stimulation for visual, women will sacrifice visual for intimate." If her husband comes to bed and touches her mind and body intimately, she will be aroused. But, if she comes to bed dressed seductively, the intimacy is not as important as just simply having the physical sexual contact. Let's face it, where it may be difficult for a man to put together all the right words, God created women with all the mental and physical ingredients necessary to instantly become sensuous and charming.

Sexual Activity for Men Is Similar to Riding a Roller Coaster

Solomon continues to describe his bride's beautiful garden being decorated with fruit that is sweet to his taste, and the fragrance of her garden has an odor that is calling him intimately. *Thy plants are an orchard of pomegranates, with pleasant fruits; henna, with spikenard, Spikenard and saffron; calamus and cinnamon, with all trees of frankincense; myrrh and aloes, with all the chief spices; Song of Solomon 4: 13–14.* It should be understood that sexual activity for men is similar to riding a roller coaster. Get in, jerked off to a quick start, jerked up and down, whooshed around quickly and, finally, jerked to a finish. The hormones in a man's body that are responsible for arousal quickly build up and then are quickly released after orgasm. Please, men, do not be offended by my description. It is important that you understand how your sexual hormones function and learn how to adjust them accordingly, during intimacy. However, for women, their arousal is similar to hiking up a mountain; it requires one step at a time to make it to the top. Hiking up a mountain requires moving slowly as you step from rock to rock being careful not to fall. It's disappointing for a women when her partner attempts to take her to the top of the mountain of intimacy too fast, eventually tiring after continuing to try, and never taking her to the top. Taking her to the top requires moving at her pace, with delicate intimate strides. Being oh so careful to skillfully move from one area of her body to the other, knowing when to take a break and linger on one part, and knowing when to continue your journey. It should be further understood that if her partner takes her to the top of the mountain of intimacy, he must also guide her back down after orgasm. By intimately leading her with hugs, kisses, soft touches and conversation. For a woman, arousal slowly builds long before it becomes a physical desire for sex.

Sexual Motivation for Women Is Similar to Taking Her for a Long Stroll up a Mountain

Before longing for sexual stimulation, a woman first needs to feel attractive and sensual. She needs to feel drawn to a man and to enjoy sharing time together. It could be days before she wants to engage in physical activity. This is where compromise plays an important role. There are times when the heat of intimacy strikes and, due to time constraints, you both prefer a "quickie" ride on the sexual roller coaster. Then there are times when you have the time and feel like taking a long intimate stroll up the mountain of intimacy together. The concern is for both partners to be agreeable. Then they may participate in the agreed upon activity together.

I have shopped with Beverly as she looked for a particular item to decorate our physical home. I was not interested in the shopping; I just went along for the ride. As we went from store to store, she would pick up an item and ask my opinion. I would always respond with, "it looks nice." However, Beverly had to mentally picture the item in the home, in the actual space and with the surrounding colors and furnishings it would be placed among. When all this had been considered, she then made her decision. When she finally chooses to purchase an item and bring it home, even though I was just along for the ride, I get to share in the beauty the item may bring in the home. It is sad to say that many relationships suffer greatly from a lack of intimate arousal because one partner was just "along for the ride," without considering the importance of his or her role. He or she takes no time to consider how to arouse the desire for sex in his or her partner, but leaves it to their partner, and just shares in the activity.

Some Partners Are Just Along for the Sexual Ride

Arousing the desire to decorate intimate can involve:

Calling your partner during the day, expressing how he or she intimately arouses you.

Extending an invitation for an evening of intimate pleasure.

Sending a card of appreciation for past sexual moments.

Preparing a warm bath with music and candles for your partner

Giving your partner the evening off to prepare for intimacy

Giving your partner his or her own evening, to enjoy whatever they want.

Spending one night touching and caressing only.

Calling your partner and telling him or her what will intimately happen later.

Making reservations at a hotel and kidnapping your partner for the night.

Observation

"Observing involves looking, listening ,and asking. Don't assume anything or interpret. If you don't understand, ask again. Then follow and act on it. Don't dismiss."

"It would help if my partner would talk to me during sex. I need to know what feels good and what does not."

"Take time to observe my pleasure, and my frustration, then make the appropriate moves during sex."

"My partner needs to understand that my body tells the whole story. Just pay attention."

The second step in setting the M.O.O.D. is observation. Observation is critical to the sexual technique used following the arousal stage. Solomon observes his wife's genital area and views it as a *"A fountain of gardens, a well of living waters, and streams from Lebanon. "Song of Solomon 4: 13–15.*

The bride becomes so secure in her husband's love that she begins to unlock her garden (vagina) and open it to him. She becomes so aroused that her vagina is symbolic of a well with fresh water waiting to fulfill the sexual thirst of her partner. The "streams flowing from Lebanon" is symbolic of vaginal secretions awaiting her husband's intimate entry.

Observe When to Stop Serving the Appetizers and Begin Serving the Main Course

While trying to create the right M.O.O.D. for intimacy, have you ever misread the signals that your partner was giving? There may have been times when arousal developed into what appears to be physically "yes," but the emotional response was "no" or "not yet." The human body can provide a number of distinctive intimate cues, but intimacy is predicated on paying close attention and acting on the right cues. Facial expressions, body movements, tone of voice, positive moans of pleasure all can be helpful signals in enhancing intimacy. Careful observation will help each partner transition the other into each phase of the lovemaking cycle. Without careful observation, you may move too quickly or too slowly, and you may sabotage your intimacy. Creating the beauty of intimate decoration requires more than just setting the stage; it requires that you absorb the feelings coming from your partner. By observing your partner's intimate needs—physical, emotional, or both will bring your relationship on one accord.

I can remember when my father began teaching me how to barbecue on the outside grill. He stated that it was important to observe the heat within the coals, not the flame surrounding them. The first time I tried it, I put the coals in the barbecue pit, lit the coals, and noticed the roaring fire. Without paying attention to the heat, I put the meat on the grill too soon and the fire went out, which meant I had to start over again. The problem was that I observed the fire from the outside and did not take the time to rub my hands over the coals to feel if there was true heat within them. Then there was an occasion in which I started with too many coals, and the fire became too hot and, this time I burned the meat by cooking it too fast. I learned that building a good fire takes time and patience. I needed to start with just a few pieces of charcoal and to add more as the inner glow of the heat began to illuminate. In the context of intimate relationships, partners must observe each other from the inside out. The passion comes from within, and when a partner fails to recognize the temperature of the passion, he or she can ruin the sexual meal. To light the heat of passion requires being able to observe when to stop serving the appetizers of foreplay and began serving the main course of sexual intercourse. The point is to be careful not to begin too soon; but don't wait too long, only to discover that the fire has burned out, and one partner may become too disgusted to start all over again.

Operation
(Orgasm Phase)

"I'm grateful that my husband is not selfish. His sexual mannerisms put my need for intimacy first."

"My wife is very sensitive to my sexual needs as a man. Even when she is not physically in the mood, she strives to satisfy my need."

"I wish my partner would take time and focus more on my responses than his technique."

"I've discovered that I must vary my sexual techniques because my wife's desire changes with each encounter."

The third stage of the M.O.O.D. is operation, or sexual technique between partners that can produce orgasm, the build-up of physical, and emotional stimulation. The orgasm that is produced through the physical operation can bring intimate excitement for both partners. Intimate operation means learning to recognize the orgasmic activity of your partner. It's similar to a couple finishing decorating a room. It is filled with the furniture and decorations they have pictured and all the colors work together. Once it is complete, they walk into the room and immediately feel the M.O.O.D. that they have worked so hard to achieve. There is a feeling of warmth, comfort, and closeness because it was a project that they worked on together, and now they share in its beauty.

In Song of Solomon 4:15, Solomon and his bride were intimately decorating their relationship. Now she responds to his beautiful words describing her M.O.O.D. In Song of Solomon 4:16, *"Awake, O north wind, and come, thou south; blow upon my garden, that its spices may flow out. Let my beloved come into his garden, and eat his pleasant fruits."* She is now aroused by his tender words of passion and invites him into her garden (vagina) by blowing, starting from the north of her body, which could be understood as her head, and slowly continuing downward south, which could be understood as her genital area, with caresses of passion. Her desire is great, and she communicates this to her husband as she prepares to give him permission to enter her garden and feast with intimate delight. The method of communicating with your partner is important. Each couple should develop of language for intimacy.

The Questions Is Sometimes Asked by Women "How Do I Know When I've Had an Orgasm?"

The orgasm phase comes in Song of Solomon 4: 16, "*I am come into my garden, my sister, my spouse. I have gathered my myrrh with my spice;* A question sometimes asked is "how does one know when he or she has experienced an orgasm?" With men, the orgasm is created through the stimulation of the penis and manifested through the ejaculation of semen. However, for women, achieving an orgasm is much different, and requires that her partner develop certain skills of operation. Without such skills, his partner will eventually become frustrated with sex.

The orgasm phase tends to be the most difficult phase because each individual responds differently to the variety of stimulations that can cause orgasms. To fully enjoy the orgasm phase requires that each partner know the identifying signs: (1) increased breathing, (2) stomach spasms, and (3) tightening of the body. Females can have more than one orgasm. The question sometimes asked by women is "how do I know when I've experienced an orgasm?" When a woman experiences an orgasm, she will know it. Your body will manifest itself differently, and a feeling will flow through your body that will become uncontrollably overwhelming. During the operation phase, each partner should develop a technique that can be shared with the other that will help increase the orgasmic phase.

The operation phase seeks to direct your intimate techniques toward assisting your partner to achieve a higher level of ecstasy. Couples have to strive to know their partners, and each intimate experience should provide a new understanding and a search for new operations.

There Should Be a Period of Teasing That Will Build Desire That Releases Itself Through Orgasm

Skillful operation requires mental thought prior to physical sex and a plan designed to decorate all areas of your partner's body so as to produce the beauty of an orgasm. It requires a period of touching physically, mentally, and spiritually. This touching should start long before partners come together physically, and there should be a period of teasing that will build desire that releases itself through orgasm. This process can be time consuming and requires focus. It should be the desire of both partners to be concerned about each other's sexual and intimate satisfaction. This means communicating before, during, and after intimacy. If your partners technique is wonderful during intimacy, communicate your feelings during that period and they will know how to stimulate the necessary areas that produce orgasms. But to leave your partner guessing during intimacy because of silence or no physical involvement is not their fault. However, it is never a good practice to fake an orgasm. Not only is faking unfair to your partner, but unfair to yourself. If any partner feels they are having problems experiencing the orgasm phase, each must be sensitive to the others lack of skill, and become willing students. But, you can't expect each other to automatically know without intimate communication and sharing. If your technique is in tune with your partners, you will know whether an orgasm is reached, or if your partner is just reaching.

As a couple, it's imperative that you create a method for communicating during intimacy, discussing the needed techniques and skills that enhance your lovemaking cycle. The purpose is for both partners to enjoy themselves, not for just one partner to be left alone in a sexual world of unknown.

Determination
(Resolution)

"Once my husband learned more about my sexual desire, he ceased becoming disappointed when he couldn't bring me to immediate orgasm. I appreciated the fact that he did not give up, but became more determined to satisfy my desire by spending more quality time during sex.

"Sometimes I wonder if she's satisfied after sex."

"I wish my partner would spend more time cuddling after sex."

The fourth stage of creating the M.O.O.D. is determination. There are times when the M.O.O.D. that has been created does not always work, and there are times when it becomes something wonderful. Never stop trying to intimately please your partner. Attempt to make each intimate experience something new and different. There will be times when a technique will not produce an orgasm for your partner, but don't take it personally. Take it as a sign that your M.O.O.D. needs more creative thought and that you should communicate better with your partner intimately.

After Sex, Partners Need to Cuddle, Talk, and Reassure Each Other's Performance

The purpose of the M.O.O.D. should never be to perfect one technique, but to work on developing many styles of pleasure that provide stimulation and enhance your home of intimacy. The M.O.O.D. should never dissipate after orgasm. The M.O.O.D. should follow with an afterglow of mutual and emotional satisfaction as the physical returns to normal. The determination should be to intimately support your partner to a smooth conclusion of intimacy, not an abrupt ending. This means that after sex, partners need to cuddle and talk. It's definitely a no-no for one partner to physically disappear or fall asleep immediately after intimacy. This makes a partner feel used and will eventually turn the partner's M.O.O.D. to resentment.

In Song of Solomon 5:1a, Solomon and his bride basked in the beauty of their intimate decoration. *I have eaten my honeycomb with my honey; I have drunk my wine with my milk. Eat, O friends.* Solomon shares in the afterglow, and God gives this couple His heavenly seal of approval of their erotic encounter.

It'a Definitely a No-No for One Partner to Physically Disappear or Fall Asleep after Intimacy Abandoning the Other

SPECIAL INTIMATE DECORATING PROJECT:

Intimately decorating together can be fun. Below are a list of intimate decorating materials, but as a couple, you are the decorators. To intimately decorate requires mental preparation to perform the physical manifestation. The ideas below incorporate both materials. If your relationship needs redecorating intimately, spend quality time together organizing materials and ideas that will beautify your home of intimacy.

Some Material That Can Be Used for Creating the M.O.O.D.

Sight	Words of Desire	Lingerie	Candles	Variety
Smell	Body Lotion	Flowers	Bathing	Massage
Taste	Whip Cream	Chocolate	Fruit	Good Manners
Hearing	Tongue	Teasing	Kissing	Warm Fire
Touching	Finger foods	Fantasies	Feathers	Contraception
Timing	Stroking	Relaxation	Music	Satin Sheets
Sensuality	Love Letters	Pillows	Prayer	Complementing

Chapter Seventeen
Intimate Security

"*He who finds a wife finds a good thing, and obtains favor from the LORD*" *Proverbs 18: 22*

"*You husbands likewise, live with your wives in an understanding way, as with a weaker vessel, since she is a woman; and grant her honor as a fellow heir of the grace of life, so that your prayers may not be hindered*" *1 Peter 3: 7*

"*An excellent wife is the crown of her husband, But she who shames him is as rottenness in his bones*" *Proverbs 12: 4*

...Intimate security, or securing your home of intimacy. The intimate relationship between a husband and wife should be considered a valuable asset. The scriptures above state that the relationship between a man and woman is full of precious gifts. When a man finds a wife, God promises that the husband will not only obtain favor from the Lord, but when his wife is treated with honor, God will also hear and answer his prayers. As for the wife, it is a benefit to be honored and loved by her husband and considered a crown of intimate completion. Intimate security between a couple consists of heartfelt feelings that exist only between a husband and wife, feelings that can only be unlocked by each other. Since these attributes are supposed to be shared between them only, there is a need to protect these intimate treasures from outside intruders. When a couple follows the blueprints, establishes a foundation, construct a frame, and decorates with intimate beauty, it is a gift. If your husband is kind and caring, or your wife is supportive and always by your side, God recognizes this type of relationship as something beautiful.

Just as security is important for a physical home, emotional security is important for intimate relationships. Couples are often naive to the fact that outsiders will lie in wait for an opportunity to rob their relationship of joy, peace, communication, intimacy, or fellowship. However, this idea is expressed in Genesis 3: 1–24. Satan entered the garden where Adam and the woman (Eve) lived in harmony as a married couple. He then robbed Adam and the woman (Eve) of their fellowship with God. God provided all the things that they needed to survive and live forever. However, God added a restriction to the relationship. *"And the Lord God took the man, and put him into the garden of Eden to till it and to keep it. And the Lord God commanded the man, saying, Of every tree of the garden thou mayest freely eat; But of the tree of the knowledge of good and evil, thou shalt not eat of it; for in the day that thou eatest thereof thou shalt surely die,"* Genesis 2: 15–17. God gave Adam and the woman (Eve) free will. However, with free will, temptation somehow follows. No matter how sincere the couple, an adversary will seek to challenge their sincerity. If there is a deviation from the couple's vows, there is a chance that the harmony between the couple will be broken.

When a couple fails to take necessary security precautions, intimacy within the home can be stolen and the relationship will suffer a great loss. Many couples have been victimized by an intruder, their relationship ransacked, leaving one or both partners feeling violated and empty. Many times partners experience this feeling of emptiness and have problems putting a finger on what is missing. In the garden of Eden, the serpent knew the rules that God had established. However, he sought to confuse the woman with deceit to test her free will. Adam and Eve felt that, because they were in paradise, they would not be subjected to temptation. The mistake was that Eve opened the door of her heart to a stranger, she provided information that God had given to her and Adam. It does not matter how spiritually strong you may be, the intruder is cunning and will deceitfully rob from the most resistant person. The serpent got Eve's attention, she entertained his conversation, and then offered her something she thought was positive, which later, had a negative affect on her marriage and relationship with God.

Consider your relationship. How much energy have you spent on its security? Have you thought of your relationship as a priceless gift of God that cannot easily be replaced? Have you ever thought about the fact that an intruder may attempt to enter your relationship and rob it of intimate valuables? Or have you been negligent and left the door open and found that a valuable piece of your relationship is now gone. The purpose of intimate security is to sustain a happy and fulfilling relationship, while at the same time protecting those feelings that produce fulfillment.

Secure Intimacy with Spiritual Observance

"Humble yourselves, therefore under the mighty hand of God, that he may exalt you in in due time, casting all your care upon him; for he careth for you. Be sober, be vigilant, because your adversary, the devil, like a roaring lion walketh about, seeking whom he may devour;" 1 Peter 5: 6–8

The step to achieving intimate security is to become spiritually observant and to understand that there is an adversary. To blindly enter into a marriage without a level of humility will often result in a prideful fall. Physical strength, education, or financial independence will not lock out the intruder. A couple needs to become spiritually prepared which means constant prayer and spiritually encouraging each other. There are times when a couple is separated due to work or other outside responsibilities. A lack of spiritual preparation can leave the one partner vulnerable when the other is not around.

*"For we wrestle not against flesh and blood, but against principalities, against powers, against the rulers of the darkness of this world, against spiritual wickedness in high places "*Ephesians 6: 12. Couples have to wrestle constantly with principalities, those ideals outside of the home that can have an effect on the inside.

"We've Got Too Much Invested in the Marriage to Throw It All Away"

To spiritually guard against the intruder doesn't require hand to hand combat or physical weapons. The intruder can be lust of the flesh, eyes, or pride of life. It can also represent problems with pornography, meddling acquaintances, new acceptable standards of living, worldly influences on children, and non-believing spouses. All of these are contributing principalities that the intruder will use as a weapon to rob a relationship of intimate security. One of the most difficult principalities that arise in some marriages is the blending of families: bringing two different families together to create one. And unless a couple realizes the challenge, their intimate relationship can be sabotaged with surprised intrusions. The best defense against the adversary is to never disagree publicly, but always be viewed as a praying couple in all circumstances. When the adversary witnesses a couple praying, it is similar to having security bars on a physical home. While the bars do not always keep the intruders out, it makes it more difficult for them to break in, and works well as a deterrent.

A woman who caught her husband in an adulterous affair and after much prayer for guidance, immediately forgave him. When asked by puzzled family and friends why she didn't divorce him, she replied, "We've got too much invested in the marriage to throw it all away."

Their investment consisted of priceless moments of emotional growth, intimate bonding, spiritually overcoming other obstacles in their relationship, and raising their children. She understood that somewhere in the past, the intimate security in their relationship had been breached, and an intruder entered in to steal her husband. This woman's attitude was that regardless of the sin of her husband, it was more important to determine why the break-in occurred and to secure that area of the relationship. She recognized there was an intimate value in her husband that no one else could see. To those on the outside looking in, the husband was junk and needed to be disposed of, but to his wife he was a valuable treasure. True, he may have been a tarnished treasure, but his wife was willing to work with him to make him shine again. This wife refused to allow the intruder to "get away" with stealing God's gift to her.

Keys to Securing Intimacy

"Let the husband render unto the wife her due; and likewise also, the wife unto the husband. The wife hath not power of her own body, but the husband; and likewise also the husband hath not power of his own body, but the wife." 1 Corinthians 7: 2–3

Keys are vital to a home's security. In a home of intimacy, God presents the husband and wife with keys, which should never be given out to anyone else. I observed a couple in which, around the wife's neck was a heart shaped charm that appeared as a lock needing a key. Around her husband's neck was the key. This couple was symbolically demonstrating that he owned the key that would open her heart, and she had a lock on her heart that could only be opened by his key. Every couple should be the only holders to the keys to their intimacy. Intimate keys are physical and emotional gifts that couples exchange between themselves.

Intimate keys are activities that can produce happiness and joy in your relationship. Keys could be described as those secret gestures or non-verbal expressions that can only be interpreted by individual couples. It's fun to secretly flirt with Beverly in the midst of a group, and never utter a word. However, there have been times when the necessary key was not flirting, but a quiet supportive spirit. Couples should always carry a set of intimate keys, specially designed to open the other's innermost heart. Keys are cut to fit a lock, and the same is true with intimate keys. At the beginning of a relationship a partner may use the wrong key, such as saying the wrong thing at the wrong time. However, as the relationship progresses, partners learn the groove of each other's needs and personality, to recognize which intimate key to use at the appropriate time. It is important to spend time with your partner to understand which key is needed for certain circumstances. There are some couples who have difficulty expressing their feelings, or communicating their needs. I would suggest that a couple keep a bell around their house, and when an intimate need arises, simply, ring the bell. I've noticed that when builders are constructing a home, and when it's time for lunch or break. There is usually a lunch truck that arrives with a loud horn to alerts the workers that its time for a break. Constructing a home of intimacy can be demanding, and when a partner rings the bell, it alerts the other that there is an intimate need to be addressed. Whether it's a supportive hug, or a kiss of reassurance, or maybe a smile of acceptance, it can be used as an intimate key.

Just a word of warning: Never give copies of your intimate keys to anyone. Those personal secrets between a couple should stay within the home and should not be shared with anyone. Some have given keys of intimacy to friends, sharing ideas about their spouse to others while they await an opportunity to use those same keys to rob their home of intimacy. A good rule would be if you don't trust anyone with keys to your physical home, don't trust them with keys to your home of inti-macy. I've witnessed individuals sharing with friends intimate activities within their relationship that was suppose to be confidential. However, this confidential information was shared with others, who now also have a copy of their intimate keys.

Intimate security should be examined regularly. It is the husband's job to ensure that his relationship is properly secured. And it is the wife's responsibility to submit to the intimate security established by her husband. God has placed man as head of his household, and it is his job to protect his relationship from unwanted intruders. After the fall in the garden, when God interrogated Adam, he blamed the incident on his wife. *And the man said, "The woman whom thou gavest to be with me, she gave me of the tree, and I ate" Genesis 3: 12.* The man who originally considered his wife as *"Bone of my bone, and flesh of my flesh"* now blamed her for something that God left as his responsibility. Men, stop leaving the door open and blaming your wife for every issue in the relationship. Remember when she is honored, so are you and the relationship. But when dishonor is brought upon the relationship, it is the husbands responsibility to go before God to restore the honor, not his wife's. And women, if he should inadvertently leave the door open, be careful not to criticize or ridicule. But continue to shelter him with love and compassion. And for God's sake, "Don't keep a hidden record of his mistakes."

It's important to realize that just as there is no fool-proof method of security for a physical home, there is none for your home of intimacy. One of the best safeguards is for a couple to keep their intimate possessions to themselves. They should not allow anyone to pry into their relationship with questions or opinions. An intruder will attempt to gain entry by using keys that look genuine or appear to fit, they are called "pick keys." The intruder will try to pick your heart with intimate phases, or pick your mind with negativity about your partner, and further attempt to pick your body with innocent hugs or holy kisses. The intruder will even pick your spiritual convictions to challenge your beliefs. It is important that a couple become aware when the intruder is using "pick keys" to intrude into their relationship.

Securing each other's emotional needs within a marriage requires that both partners work at understanding each other. During counseling, I have heard couples describe occasions when they have walked into a room with their partner and felt that the atmosphere was "chilly." When your home of intimacy has a "chilly" atmosphere, stop and check to make sure their are no outside drafts. An outside draft are those circumstances that come blowing into your relationship. It could occur in any room of the home, especially the bedroom. To keep the door closed to others means showing sensitivity and observing those things that are important to your partner that you may not view as important. I know a woman who spent a great deal of time improving her body at her health club. Her goal was to lose weight and tone her body. After months of rigorous exercise, her body showed progress. Everyone around her, except her husband, noticed her physical improvements. While she appreciated the compliments of others, she still felt an emotional emptiness from her husband. Most importantly, he failed to recognize the need of his wife to have him notice. As a consequence, she filled her emotional needs with others outside of the home. Her husband needed to put aside those things that were blinding his view of his wife's need for emotional support.

It is also important to understand that every individual requires a different level of emotional security. Just as there are different body temperatures, there are different emotional temperatures. If your partner needs to be told on a regular basis, "I love you," then say it. Then there are partners who are not quite as "touchy". Whatever it takes to maintain a level of comfort and warmth within your home of intimacy should be done and balanced between both partners.

Some couples describe themselves as having "drifted apart." When partners in a relationship "drift apart," it means that, somehow, the door has been left open and the winds of separation has blown them apart. This is similar to both partners relying on the other to keep the door shut. A couple should never depend only on the other. To maintain the intimate part of their relationship, both partners should work at initiating intimacy. They should stand together and watch together because, ultimately, it does not matter who leaves the door open, but that it has been left open, and needs to be closed.

What is important is to pay attention to your relationship. A woman who constantly ignores her husband's need for sex is "leaving the door open." A husband who finds great pleasure in his work and pays his wife no attention is "leaving the door open." A woman who can't find the words to edify her husband is "leaving the door open." A husband finds no need to compliment his wife is "leaving the door open." When you neglect your relationship, you "leave the door open." When the door is left open, you expose your home of intimacy and make it vulnerable to unwanted entry.

In Case of an Intimate Intrusion

There may be a time during your relationship that an intruder enters your relationship and robs it of intimate valuables. Relationships are often full of misunderstandings and one's partner can be caught off guard and fall into temptation. If you find an intrusion has taken place, the problem will not be solved by finger pointing and finding fault, but only by love and compassion. *"Brethren, even if a man is caught in any trespass, you who are spiritual, restore such a one in a spirit of gentleness; each one looking to yourself, lest you too be tempted" Galations 6: 1.* When a physical home has been robbed, one needs to call the police. Similarly, when your relationship falls victim to the adversary, call on God and pray that He will help you to secure your relationship in the future and restore your intimate valuables. This will take time and a great deal of energy. However, working together, you can ensure that your intimate security is never breached again.

Lock It up:

Is your home of intimacy securely locked up with intimate ideas, thoughts, and feelings? Or is there a sense of insecurity. Spend time thinking about ways to intimately secure your relationship or evaluate your current feelings. Just think, when was the last time flowers were sent to your partner? How do you greet each other at the end of the day? or Can you look deeply into each others eyes and feel secure. Share those little things that were once special, that may have been inadvertently neglected over time.

Chapter Eighteen
Preventive Maintenance

"Confess your faults one to another, and pray one for another, that ye may be healed. The effectual, fervent prayer of a righteous man availeth much" James 5: 16.

The longevity of an intimate relationship is dependent upon a certain amount of preventive maintenance. For a couple to maintain continuous happiness in their home of intimacy means taking time together to strengthen areas of their relationship. A physical home requires that the owners take time to routinely check the premises for possible internal and external problems. To maintain a home of intimacy means that both partners be concerned about all issues involving their relationship. There are times when early detection of small problems can be easily repaired before they become major problems.

One of the best preventive maintenance tips is the ability to pray for your relationship on a daily basis. This means praying for yourself, your partner, and your marriage. There are a group of wives in my church who started a weekly prayer line over the phone to pray for their husbands and their marriages. Daily prayer helps to strengthen us and also provides spiritual optimism in the face of problematic situations. When a couple prays together, they yield themselves and their relationship to God.

"Praying with my wife helps me to understand her needs for our marriage. It also provides the opportunity for us to come together, on one accord, sharing our need before the Lord."
                                                            Walter and Yolanda

"Praying together with my partner helps change our hearts and attitudes, that were different before we bowed down on our knees. I love hearing my husband praying for me, I can feel the intimacy and sincerity in his heart."   *Roy and Denise*

"Praying with my wi.fe helps us share a common bond."
                                                            John and Traci

"I find that praying with my husband brings us together as one mind sharing each others needs."   *Linda and William*

"Praying together brings a closeness in our relationship, becoming one as well as building spiritual strength."   *Davil and Beverly*

These testimonials demonstrate that prayer in a relationship can be a meaningful and fulfilling experience. Intimacy also can be found in spiritual oneness. When a couple ceases to pray on a regular basis, the focus of building a home of intimacy can become lost.

Preventing Structural Cracks
(Problems with Phileo Love)

If at any point in your relationship a partner feels a separation involving intimate friendship or abandonment, the importance is to come together and close the gap. To allow a separation to continue means that it will become wider with time. When an intimate separation becomes too wide, outside elements can find their way into the relationship.

Preventive Maintenance Would Go the Heart of a Problem and Solve It from Inside out

Too often a partner will relate his or her feelings in attempting to bring to light and solve what he or she feels is a problem, and their partner will respond; " I don't see this as being a problem, so there's nothing to resolve." In a relationship that uses preventive maintenance, partners will work with each other to locate the problem, and help solve it. Many relationships have had major problems due to minor misunderstandings from an unresolved past problem. Preventive maintenance goes to the heart of the problem and attempt to solve it from the inside out.

Displaced feelings, harsh words, neglect, and past hurts all attribute to cracks being formed in the structure of Phileo love. I had a couple in counseling and, after several sessions, the wife admitted that she was suffering from a past hurt related to her marriage. She expressed that hurt in counseling to her husband and simply wanted an explanation from her husband regarding the issue. The wife felt a separation that stemmed from an incident in their relationship years ago. She spent several years trying to ignore the issue, but within the hurt still remained. The husband had the tools he needed to repair the problem. He needed to provide his wife with his attention and concern about resolving the issue. However, instead of trying to repair it, he became resentful and defensive. He felt it was in the past. He didn't quite understand that "sometimes to be satisfied without, is to be unsatisfied within." He wanted her to be satisfied with the present condition of their marriage, but she was still unsatisfied and concerned about the future. He just did not understand that his home of intimacy needed some repairing. Sure, it was still standing, but for how long? In a relationship, to put off today can often result in no tomorrow.

Sometimes to Be Satisfied Without, Is to Be Unsatisfied Within

Repairing the separation in your friendship takes time, effort, and a willingness to patch the crack of separation by falling in love all over again. To properly repair phileo love means taking the time to fill in the missing pieces. With so many other activities involved in a relationship, specialized intimacy needs can often be easily overlooked. I hear the same statement on a regular basis from both men and women. "Why don't you do the things you use to do?" They want to know what happened to those special intimate acts, moments, and feelings that brought them together as friends, and lovers. Preventive maintenance would seek to restore those intimate acts, moments and feelings from the past on a regular basis. Asking your partner out on a date, or sneaking away for a weekend, even after marriage is still appropriate. What's even more special would be to write a letter or send of card of sincere appreciation for your partner being who he or she is.

In a Relationship, to Put off Today Can Often Result in No Tomorrow

The spark of friendship is similar to the pilot light used in gas stoves. The pilot light is a small flame that constantly burns within the stove. Once the stove is turned on, the pilot light ignites a big flame for cooking. However, if the pilot light is accidentally blown out, one cannot light the big flame. Preventive maintenance works to keep the pilot light burning. It's not necessarily the big things, but the small things that are remembered and keep the small fire burning. I have heard some women say that it doesn't matter whether they receive a dozen roses; they would be happy with just one rose. One rose signifies that their partner took time to think about them. Men don't always remember the big gifts that were given, but do remember the time that their wife spontaneously gave him a sensuous body massage. It's the thought that really keeps the romantic spark burning within the heart.

Preventative Maintenance Works to Keep the Pilot Light Burning

Preventing Plumbing Problems (Communication)

Plumbing Back-up (No Communication)

One of the biggest preventive maintenance measures in a home of intimacy is to maintain the flow of communication. When the flow of communicate stops, everything in the household is affected. When a couple fails to communicate, there is no understanding, harmony, peace, or intimacy. They may have physical sex as a duty, but there will not be pleasure. I have heard of couples, experiencing a period in which they were not communicating. They continued sex only to keep their partners from straying outside of the marriage.

When there is no communication between a couple, it is similar to the plumbing in a physical home being shut-down. The occupants in the home may have to go other places to use the facilities of others. Providing preventive maintenance in your communication means talking when things are wonderful and talking even more when things are not. It is never a good practice to get opinions from those other than your partner, unless that person is a qualified professional. When there is a major plumbing problem in your home, you don't call anyone other than a plumber. To call anyone else may cause a bigger problem. Many couples have paid a high emotional price for not attending to their communication needs. There are times when the communication back-up seems impossible to work through. It requires that couples work together to clear the back-up. Clearing the back-up means: (1) praying for direction, (2) discussing the issues that caused the communication back-up, and (3) using the scriptures as a protective coating against future communication back-ups.

Low Pressure Plumbing
(Partial Communication)

The force of water through pipes makes the water more effective. To try and shower with the water pressure very low defeats the purpose. The purpose of a shower is to provide a "zest," something that is warm, soothing, and often therapeutic.

One partner not providing sufficient communication is similar to having low pressure plumbing. When one partner feels the need to share something important, and the other is not paying attention, there will be misunderstandings. A relationship with a low-flow communication problem can leave a partner unfulfilled. Mutual communication can fill emotional emptiness, provide edifying therapy to the mind and spirit, and wake-up a sleeping intimate relationship.

Constant Plumbing Drip
(Nagging Communication)

If one partner is a nagging person, he or she will disturb the flow of communication. A constant dripping faucet is not only annoying, but wasteful, and over time, leaves a permanent rust stain in the sink. A relationship full of nagging will eventually cause one partner to become annoyed. If the nagging continues on a regular basis, it will leave a stain of resentment. If your relationship is suffering from nagging communication, take a moment to think about whether the nagging really works. If your answer is no, then seek other ways of positive communication. A partner cannot be changed by nagging, but can be changed with a little creative communication. There was a woman who was concerned about her husband's health because he was gaining too much weight. She spent an exceptional amount of time nagging him about his diet. She finally realized that the nagging failed and that her husband was becoming resentful and irritated. After a little creative thinking, she decided to quit the nagging and began fixing his plate for him. This served two purposes for the husband: (1) he no longer was being nagged, and (2) he was so elated with the tender loving care shown by his wife that he did not notice the smaller portions of food on his plate. She was fulfilled and so was her husband. However, if your answer is that your partner does respond to nagging, then ask yourself what kind of mental stain you are leaving on your partner. He or she may respond to the nagging, but what is your partner thinking about you when he or she responds? The purpose of a fulfilling relationship is for partners to feel and think positive about serving each other. For a partner to feel and think otherwise is the opposite of the goal of mutual communication.

A Partner Can't Be Changed by Nagging, But Can Be Changed with a Little Creative Communication

When a faucet continues to drip, there are usually two solutions. There is something missing on the inside, such as a washer, that can stop the drip. If that does not solve the problem, you can replace the whole faucet. When a partner does not recognize the need to repair his or her nagging attitude, then the other may eventually start looking for a new partner to replace the old nagging one.

Energy Overload
(Quality Time Problems)

I began feeling my wife had an intimate energy shortage about the sixth month of our first pregnancy and for several months after the birth of our first child. I found it difficult to understand the change, because within me, I didn't change, my desire was the same. So, what happened to her? Not being a woman, nor understanding the energy involved in becoming a new mother was mentally draining in itself. It wasn't that her desire was not there, but just no energy. However, as a man I had a need for intimacy. That personal attention I had once received prior to the new baby had suddenly stopped. The time came when I had to creatively think of a way to draw her attention toward me without neglecting our son. Since my wife worked full time also, I found myself beginning to perform routine household duties for my son before my wife arrived home. Since I had more energy, it was my intent to complete whatever tasks needed to be done, and my wife wouldn't have to exert any physical energy. When she arrived home, my son was fed, bathed, and dinner cooked. This practice allowed us to spend intimate quality time, which didn't always include sexual intercourse, just personal attention that we both needed. This experience taught me maturity and enabled me to understand that my role as a husband and father stretched far beyond just "bringing home the bacon role, but taking the time to cook it also.   *Philip*

When I was in elementary school, I was taught home fire prevention methods. I can vividly remember the firemen teaching about the "electrical octopus." This is where too many appliances are plugged into one outlet at the same time. An "electrical octopus" can cause an electrical energy shortage or start a fire. Either one would be dangerous if occurred.

Putting Other Activities First can Result in an "Intimacy Burn out"

A relationship also should be routinely checked for an intimate energy shortage. An intimate energy shortage can be caused by too many outside activities plugged into a relationship at one time. An intimately balanced relationship requires quality time and energy. To put other activities first, while leaving your partner last, can result in an "intimacy burn out." I have witnessed couples spending too much time on other activities and neglecting their intimate relationship. When they finally decided to spend quality intimate time together, they were too tired due to an energy overload. This energy overload problem is sometimes manifested in sexual relations. If one partner finds himself or herself too tired for intimate sexual relations, the other partner will often take it personally and become resentful.

In a carefully maintained relationship, partners will recognize when there is an energy shortage. Sometimes the energy shortage is not a result of activities outside of the relationship, but demands inside the relationship.

1. If there is an intimacy energy shortage in your relationship as a result of outside activities, take time to evaluate the priority of these activities and "unplug" those that are not necessary.

2. If the energy shortage is a result of activities within the home, take a personal interest in your partner's well-being and help in whatever area in which you can save your partner's energy for intimacy. This may mean doing household chores, cooking, or helping with the children.

Exterior Maintenance
(Exterior Behavior)

The exterior appearance of a home is often crucial in determining its value. When the exterior paint is chipping or the yard is brown and full of weeds, it appears that the owners have a lack of pride or concern about their property. When the exterior of a home is not maintained, it also brings down the value of the other homes in the neighborhood.

The exterior maintenance of a marriage relationship can be crucial in providing marriage with a value to those who feel it has none. A couple who engages in unseemly behavior, or appear outwardly unhappy is similar to failing to maintain the outside appearance of a home. A couple must always be careful and observant of their surroundings. There are always those outside of the relationship observing and watching how a couple maintains themselves during certain situations. Those that observe them often based their ideas of marriage on what they view from other couples. A couple who maintains appropriate behavior outside of their home can set a good example to those who are either married or wondering if marriage is worth the effort.

True Respect and Love Can Not Continue in the Midst of Disrespect and Confusion

There will be disagreements and misunderstandings outside of the home, but to embarrass your partner in a public forum is blatantly disrespectful and reduces the value of a marriage relationship to others around. There should be a method of maintaining appropriate and respectful behavior outside of the home of intimacy. There should be an agreed upon statement or facial expression that determines "let's talk about it when we get home." While it is understandable that each partner handles anger differently, the goal is to resolve it decently and in order.

Some have asked, "why shouldn't married couples go to bed angry?" The main reason is that there is no guarantee that you both will wake-up the next morning to resolve the disagreement and apologize. The same applies when leaving home in the morning. It's important to resolve the disagreement because unforeseen circumstances could keep you apart forever. I have seen both husbands and wives who are now widowers and widows, who have problems coping with their deceased partner's death because the last conversation they had was an unresolved argument. They wrestle within themselves as to why they found it so difficult to say, "I'm sorry" to what is now perceived as a disagreement that was not worth the empty space that their partner once occupied. True respect and love cannot continue in the midst of disrespect and confusion.

One mistake I made when I began my first Christian counseling session was to assume that Christian couples could sit and discuss their differences without disrespecting each other. My first couple was a challenge, because once they got started, it became difficult to maintain order in the session. They had no respect for each other, their relationship, or what I thought of their relationship. When the session was over, I needed counseling from the pastor. I learned from that experience and from the pastor never to assume, but to present ground rules at the beginning of every counseling session.

There are times when assistance is needed in controlling behavior in a marriage during disagreements. When this occurs it is time to take a break, cool off, and pray about the issue. Prayer is vital in the maintaining of a relationship. What is important is learning how to resolve the disagreement and, at the same time edify God, your partner, and the marriage. The key to edifying anyone is the ability to pray for that person and lift your relationship to God. *Praying always with all prayer and supplication in the Spirit, and watching there unto with all perseverance and supplication for all saints. Ephesians 6:18* When you pray three things could occur:

(1) God will repair you, (2) God will repair your partner, or (3) God will repair you both together. When God repairs your relationship, His purpose is *that he might cleanse it with the washing of water by the word; That he might present it to himself a glorious Church, not having spot, or wrinkle, or any such thing; but that it should be holy and without blemish. Ephesians 5: 26–27.*

Clean up Your Actions:

A good maintenance program requires that a couple constantly observe each other and become sensitive to the behavior of their partner. Have you recognized a difference in your partners attitude or feelings related to your relationship? This project requires that both partners spend one week observing the behavior of the other. This includes asking questions and exchanging responses for the purpose of skillfully understanding your partner to avoid future maintenance problems.

Appendix I

"Can You Handle the Truth?"

To comfortably build a strong and sturdy home of marital intimacy, it requires that both partners start with a foundation of truth. Listed below are a few questions related to personal, sexual, financial, family and religious issues. The purpose is to think carefully when involving yourself in a relationship, and to review issues that may have an effect on a long term relationship. These questions should be used as a guide for pertinent information, not just for personal interrogation. Whereas some individuals will answer these questions honestly, there are those that will not. The key to handling to truth is to not only hear it, but also observe it.

GENERAL/PERSONAL:
Is there a history of mental illness in your family?
Do you have a problem with jealousy?
How many children do you currently have?
How many times have you been married?
Are you currently married?
Do you like pets?
Will you treat me the same after marriage?
What if I gain weight?
Will you give up cigarettes for our relationship?
Will you give up drinking alcohol for our relationship?
What's your present career goal?

Do you have your own place to live?

What's your feeling on possibly relocating?

What if our jobs have conflicting schedules?

Will you support my goals?

How would you feel about me working with someone of the opposite sex?

What is your favorite color?

Will you tell me if I should hurt your feelings?

Do you want a small or large wedding?

Will I have priority over your personal friends?

How will your ex effect our relationship?

If I am ever insecure, what will you do to make me feel secure?

Think, are you being compared to a lost love?

Are you on the rebound?

Do I remind you in any way of your former partner?

What's your feeling about a wife working outside of the home?

What is it that really connects us?

Do you love yourself?

Will you support me if I want to go back to school later?

What makes your life worth living?

Do you enjoy gambling?

Are you spoiled?

Do you trust me?

Will you forgive me unconditionally should I make a mistake?

Can you be patient and help me when I don't know?

Will you respect me as a man/woman?

Are you spontaneous?

Do you like a change or things to remain the same?

Will you run home to your mother every time we have a disagreement?

Can we both share in household chores?

Will we be able to share a home, but have our own space?

Do you believe in punctuality?

How important is personal appearance?
What types of entertainment do you most enjoy (movies, plays, concerts)?
Do you enjoy dancing?
Tell me something good about yourself.
What makes you the most angry?
Are you an early bird or night owl?
Is my ethnicity a problem?
How will your family and friends deal with our inter-racial relationship?
Do you have a problem sharing your feelings?
Will you be honest or lie just to satisfy me?
What makes your life worth living?
Are you ready to settle down, and why me?
What are your pet-peeves?
What lifestyle are you accustomed to living?
Do you feel you have a passive personality?
Do you feel you have a dominate personality?
Would you feel comfortable if I, as your wife bring home more money?
Do you have a history of spousal abuse?
Are you a victim of child abuse?
Can your love remain the same from day to day?
Why do you love me?
Do you cook?
If you could improve your personality, what would it be?
What are your marriage fears?
If we can't solve a problem, what will we do?
Do I sometimes embarrass you in public?
Are you comfortable with a long distance relationship?
Do you get angry when things don't go your way?
What does " I do" mean to you?
Have you ever had a broken heart?

How do you deal with the death of a loved one?
Do you have a prison record?
Have you considered our cultural differences?
Why didn't you marry your child's mother/father?
Does our difference in age matter to you?
Does the size of an engagement ring matter to you?

SEXUALITY:
Are you gay/lesbian?
Were you born male/female?
What are your sexual expectations?
What's your idea of intimacy?
Do you have a problem with cuddling?
How important is a fulfilling sexual relationship?
Do you have any apprehensions about sex?
Does the thought of sex frighten you?
What are your feelings on oral sex?
How serious is adultery to you?
What if I want sex everyday?
Would you enjoy wearing sexy lingerie for your partner?
What are some of your sexual fantasies?
Do you believe in sex before marriage?
Are you insecure about your sexuality?
What is our method of contraception?
Have you been tested for STDs?
Does your health inhibit sexual functioning?
Do you enjoy pornographic material?
Does penis size matter to you?
Do you believe in abortions?
What happens if we can't conceive children?

FINANCES:
Are you ready to settle down and support a family?
What is our plan for handling household finances?
Do you currently have any get rich quick ideas and need money?
Do you owe any money?
What's your feeling on borrowing money from others?
Are you in debt? How much?
Do you believe in saving money?
What's your feeling on pre-nuptial agreements?
Do you owe the IRS money
Do you use credit cards frequently?
Do you have a job, and what kind?
How much money do you make?

FAMILY:
How important is family time?
What is our plan of care for our aging parents?
What if an unexpected pregnancy occurs?
How many children do we plan to have?
What would be your reaction if my parents do not approve of you?
What is our plan for disciplining our children?
What if we can't have children?
How is your relationship with your immediate family?
How and where will we celebrate holiday events?
How committed are you to not exposing our children to unsavory family members?
What is your feeling on spanking children for discipline purposes?

RELIGION:
What is your idea of a Godly spouse?
How long have you been a Christian?
Do believe in the power of prayer?
What is your religious belief or foundation?

Do you believe in God?
How do we know God put us together?
Tell me about your Christian testimony.
If from different religious backgrounds, how will it effect the children?
Do you have a personal relationship with God?
Do you believe in the Bible?
How would you feel if we decided to attend different churches?
Do you have a problem with paying tithes in church?